Winning With Words

Powerful Professional Presentations

by Lis Manson

Winning With Words
Copyright © 2017 Lis Manson

Limits of Liability and Disclaimer of Warranty

The author and publisher shall not be liable for your misuse of the enclosed material. This book is strictly for informational and educational purposes only.

Warning – Disclaimer

The purpose of this book is to educate and entertain. The author and/or publisher do not guarantee that anyone following these techniques, suggestions, tips, ideas, or strategies will become successful. The author and/or publisher shall have neither liability nor responsibility to anyone with respect to any loss or damage caused, or alleged to be caused, directly or indirectly by the information contained in this book.

ISBN: 978-1-77277-165-7

Publisher

10-10-10 Publishing
Markham, ON
Canada

Printed in Canada and the United States of America

| Acknowledgements |

On the business side, I want to thank **Roberto Lloren** for shedding light on my public speaking skills and encouraging me to share the principles of delivering powerful, persuasive and professional presentations with the rest of the world. His guidance gave me the confidence to believe in my passion and launch *Winning With Words.*

I am also grateful to **Basim** and **Ramsha Mirza** of Mirza International, who accompanied me on the journey to creating *Winning With Words.*

Also, I want to thank **Miriam Cohen**, the backbone of this project, who helped me organise all this material and convert it into a valuable tool. Many thanks, too, to **Raymond Aaron** and his staff for helping this book become a reality.

| What People Are Saying About |
Lis Manson and
Winning With Words

"Thank you so much for the invitation to your Winning With Words workshop. I found it very valuable and applied the techniques that you taught at my next networking meeting, with great success. I'm sure I'm not the only one that found it valuable. I really appreciated the focus on multiple aspects of presentations as so much of a successful presentation is about the audience and the message, but most of us only focus on the slides. I think everyone can benefit from this because even a job interview is a presentation of sorts, and we all have to do those from time to time."

- Adrian Blake, Retirement Income Specialist

"When I was asked to review the Winning With Words online programmes, I didn't know what to expect. However, once I got to the actual content both courses, Become a Powerful Speaker and Master the Art of Presentations, definitely delivered. I have previously taken a couple of Public Speaking courses, as well as attended Toastmasters meetings, but the former were unnecessarily long and convoluted, and the Toastmasters meetings, although a great dive-in-head-first practice, were of little help in regards to the how-to education.

Winning With Words has created a great and useful course that's easy to understand and follow. I've learned how to better understand and connect with the audience, and then successfully drive the speaker's message and action. I've learned simple yet very effective ways to genuinely increase persuasion. And, I've learned simple but powerful tricks to improve the delivery – including how to manage arms, gestures and eyes, and how to make presentation slides stand out.

The content is interesting, engaging, thought provoking, and fulfillingly simple. The included well-chosen visual examples as well as the presentation itself, effectively illustrate the learning points. I highly recommend this course to anyone who wishes to improve his or her public speaking skills, but also to enhance everyday communication skills – and ultimately Win With Words."
- Kamil C Kowalski, Energy Shiatsu at PracticalWellness.ca

"Lis is a person who can bring out the best in you. If public speaking or presenting is a challenge for you or someone you know, Lis is the person you want to be referred to and will want to work with to advance."
- Richard Birchall, Independent Business Owner

"I highly recommend Winning With Words. Lis Manson is an engaging speaker and stands out from the rest with her personal and easily relatable style. ... I learned so much from Winning With Words and now feel more confident to speak in front of audiences of any background and size."
- Mike Aquan-Assee, Graphic Designer

"Excellent guidance in communication. Lis is a brilliant coach and mentor."
- Samia Manson, Programme Office Manager, KPMG London U.K.

"The content, format of Winning With Words are A+."
- Karen Cunningham, Lawyer

"Lis delivers ten times fifty in value helping to improve people's performance."
- Steven Klugman

"Lis always presents with confidence, clarity, wit and wisdom."
- Lynn Gauthier

| Foreword |

This book is about to immeasurably change the way you communicate for the better. Whether you are a seasoned presenter looking to up your game, or a first-time speaker feeling insecure about presenting before a large crowd, *Winning With Words* will help you hone your skills and become a confident, comfortable and effective speaker.

The ability to present ideas and convince others of their worth is at the heart of all success, whether it is in your business or in your personal life. In order to be a great speaker, you must use your words wisely but, more importantly, make yourself relatable to your audience. In doing so, you will clearly and convincingly position yourself as someone who is there to help, a partner, and not a self-serving salesperson or an adversary.

As someone who is in demand to speak all over the world, I can assure you that you can learn to be a great presenter. But, as in all things, you need to learn from the best, and Lis Manson has curated an excellent primer that lays out everything from the elementary principles of speaking to the advanced techniques that can make you a superstar communicator. There are also practical and purposeful tools for quelling the jitters that you will find useful, no matter what level speaker you are.

I cannot promise that you will become a great speaker overnight, but I can assure you that reading *Winning With Words* is the first step in getting there.

Loral Langemeier
Five-Time Bestselling Author (The Millionaire Maker), Speaker, Wealth Coach, and CEO & Founder of Live Out Loud, Inc.

| Table of Contents |

| Introduction |

Why worry about being an excellent presenter when you have so many other things to deal with? Today, presenting an idea, recommendation, story, sales pitch or just about anything you can think of is an integral part of being a good businessperson. Presenting exceptionally well is a valuable skill that helps you influence people and accomplish more. It is often how you get seen and recognised by others for your work. And, that recognition often leads to promotions and growth of income, as well as more opportunities to present.

In addition, having a well-prepared presentation and communicating it persuasively is a powerful skill. It eliminates any lingering friction between you and the members of your audience. When people can see that you care about their needs and value their time, they will want to support you. People will adopt your ideas and actually have the momentum to carry them out. You will close more deals and become an influencer of people. In short, it will help you go further in your organisation and your career.

This book will help you create Powerful Professional Presentations. You will learn what goes into a powerful presentation, and then how to craft it in a charismatic way. After that, you will learn how to present it professionally, in an authentic manner that creates a WOW factor with your audience.

This is not a coursebook or a manual; it is more of a conversation, which is to say it is filled with interesting stories and serves as a dialogue between us that can help unlock the passion of who you are. During this transformation, I will help you do something you fear, or to at least speak better than you do now, by shining a light on what you need to know and understand.

To paraphrase Marianne Williamson, we're afraid of our own light, and we keep ourselves small. Allow me to lend you some light until you become larger than you are now.

CHAPTER I
COMMON PROBLEMS THAT KEEP US FROM BEING GREAT PRESENTERS

| Chapter I - Common Problems That Keep Us From Being Great Presenters |

There may be many reasons why you are an uncertain or less than perfect presenter; however, most likely you have experienced one or more of the most common problems speakers face. Let's start by reviewing them, so you can better understand what this book is meant to banish from your life.

| Failing to Understand Body Language |

It was 1960 and history was about to be made. Richard Nixon and John F. Kennedy Jr. were to appear in the first televised presidential debate in America. An estimated 70 million viewers tuned in to watch this debate. At the conclusion of the debate, those watching on television firmly believed Kennedy to be victorious while radio listeners resolutely held that Nixon had won.

What was the reason for this discrepancy in viewpoints? How did the medium in which it was presented have such an effect on the perceived outcome? The audio was the same. Therefore the difference had to have come from what people saw. On television, Nixon appeared nervous and uncertain, while Kennedy seemed to be calm and confident. It was these body language differences that changed how people viewed the debate. Although Nixon's words may have resonated more with the audience, it was how Kennedy held and presented himself that made him the victor in the eyes of those who watched the debate instead of only listening.

Body language blunders in the early seconds of the debate set a negative tone for Nixon, from which he never recovered. He triggered distrust instantly when he did not make eye contact with the audience and, instead, turned to look at Kennedy, making him the alpha candidate.

Nixon also revealed his nervousness by tightly gripping the arm of his chair while his clenched fist displayed aggression. These visual gestures show the power of nonverbal cues. Recognising this, Nixon remarked later, "I should have remembered that a picture is worth a thousand words."

Source: historychannel.com

Body language has such a profound influence on all aspects of our life that the role it plays is critical when presenting. Changing your body position and posture can induce chemical changes in your body that make you feel more confident. And, as we saw with Nixon, good presentations can easily crumble when a presenter says one thing yet projects an entirely different message with their body. Unsuccessful body language can make you lose. However, successful body language can make you win.

Scientific research proves the importance of understanding and controlling your body language. In 1872 Charles Darwin published The Expression of the Emotions in Man and Animals and popularised scientific research and theory on nonverbal communication. A theory known as Mehrabian's Rule of Communication suggests that the emotional content of a message relies only seven percent on words, 38% on tone of voice, and a massive 55% on body language.

| Suffering From Lack of Confidence |

When it comes to having confidence, the biggest issue presenters face is that they know they are going to be critiqued and judged; they may even be ridiculed or rejected. We can all lose our confidence in such a situation; however, there is good news: it is merely in our heads. That means you can reject those thoughts and replace them with something more useful and purposeful.

In a TED talk called "The Surprising Secret to Speaking with Confidence," Caroline Goyder told a powerful and moving story about how people are able to rise to the occasion and speak publically despite the circumstances [1]:

The third lesson which is the big one is the one that really makes a difference. I started to think about this lesson a couple of weeks ago because someone I have worked with wrote to me. She wrote me an email and she said, she had been through the worst possible thing that you can imagine happening to someone. She had just got married and was on her honeymoon when her husband had a heart attack and died. She had to go back to the church in which they had recently got married and speak a eulogy for this man. In fact, she also read a poem that she had written when they first met.

She said on the worst day of my life I had to pull myself together. I had to find the energy of celebration of this man that I really loved and the only way to do it was what you taught me, the skills of breathing low and slow, taking my time, getting the control, finding my inner confidence. It was the greatest gift I could give him.

[1] http://singjupost.com/the-surprising-secret-to-speaking-with-confidence-by-caroline-goyder-full-transcript/2/

There are moments in our lives where we have to speak not because we have something to say for us, but because we want to speak for someone else. I would suggest that in those moments these skills matter more than ever. What you need to know is in those moments it is about drawing breath. It's air.

Why does air matter? It's because we breathe our thoughts. All speech is OUT BREATH. All song is out breath. And all in breath is thought. Just put a hand back on your diaphragm for a moment and breathe out. Then feel the breath in and as you breathe in think of someone you really love. Now if we were all to speak on the OUT breath, it would be full of love. Now breathe in again and breathe in a feeling of excitement for the day that is to come. If we were to breathe in and speak on that feeling we have excitement in our voices.

So you can control your voice with the idea of breath is thought. And it is in Latin – the two worlds ancient and modern. The Romans understood this; inspiration and respiration have the same root. The Romans understood that we breathe our thoughts. Because we speak on the out breath, all you have to think about is the in breath. You know the simplest way to think about the in breath is to close your mouth.

Who would have thought that the big secret that I promised you was that if you want confidence in speech all you have to do is to know when to shut your mouth? Thank you.

Plus, why do we think that just because we speak every day, we will automatically be good at doing presentations or any other kind of public speaking? They are not the same thing. Until we acknowledge there are many skills involved in speaking publically, there is no hope of positive change.

In my experience, confidence comes with something simple: practice. Being willing to practise your presentation long enough to become proficient in these new skills goes a long way in building your confidence.

And, if you keep practising until your new skills become second nature, you will begin to influence the audience rather than always having them influence how you feel about your abilities.

When you can stay incredibly focused while doing a presentation, you will do it as well as you did when you were practising in front of the bathroom mirror. You will also come full circle and put your focus back on the audience and on influencing them to adopt your Big Idea. Now, that is true confidence.

Unfortunately, getting rid of the lack of confidence is not as easy as it sounds. Confidence actually has several stages:

1. Being uncomfortable

2. Reaching past that discomfort to take some kind of action

3. Practising that action until the discomfort goes away

4. Practising and accessing your inner energy until you go beyond comfort, and actually enjoy the action

5. Embracing the action and showing your inner energy to the audience

My experiences teaching drama for many years have familiarised me with this process. I had one student whose parents were not sure about enrolling him. He had dyspraxia— clumsy syndrome — and he tried incredibly hard to play soccer with his classmates despite having "two left feet." Humiliation and being made fun of made him very depressed, so much so he didn't want to live. He was ten. Matthew was enrolled to try two classes, and I knew that he was probably verbal and auditory rather than being a visual thinker. This proved to be the case. It was as though he was given permission to become himself in an environment that helped him grow. All of his fears were put aside, and Matthew continued to become a wonderful student in the class for several years. I loved watching his positive attitude and enjoyment.

One method of teaching and practising confidence is by using improvisational (ad lib) activities. In a recent workshop, I set up a pretend cocktail party (with each person holding an imaginary glass in one hand) as an example of how to make up a story. During this imaginary cocktail party, each person in the audience had to go around to three people and talk about a success they had had in the previous two weeks. I may have had to give them a sentence now and then to get them past their initial reluctance to speak. However, that is how we teach confidence.

I also knew a man who always stuttered when he spoke. After many years practising speaking in front of others in an environment where he felt safe, he eliminated the stutter completely. He became used to overcoming his fear of speaking with a good deal of confidence. However, he also had a habit of shuffling back and forth from one foot to another when he was speaking. This was something he did in everyday life as well. Again, practising in this safe and trusting environment helped him overcome the "shuffling" and he able to stand still when speaking. It was all thanks to practising speaking in front of others that achieved his success and removed the fear.

Practice has the ability to take you from the uncomfortable to the comfortable in just about anything you do. You know, however, that because fear is an important survival signal in nature, it will never completely go away. You can, as I have shown, learn how to respond to it effectively so that it no longer impedes you.

| Misusing Your Inner Energy |

In its purest form, communication is all about energy. Without a baseline of energy simmering within us, we will be ineffective. If you do not let energy out when you present, your message will never reach your audience. During my time as a choral conductor I came to understand fully that to do that job effectively, you need to have a fire inside you.

Why? It takes a tremendous amount of energy to conduct; you need to energise the choir sufficiently so they can bounce your energy out to the audience. Similarly, you need to expend your own energy to make your audience's energy grow in the same way that the choir has to perform the music with drama and passion.

How does this happen? Let's use tuning forks as an example. When one is struck, the vibration it creates causes sound waves which strike the second tuning fork, duplicating the vibration of the original. This is called resonance. Since vibrations and sound waves are just different forms of energy, they are linked.

The same process applies to you and your audience, with whom you are linked. To truly resonate with them during your presentations, your voice and body language have to successfully transfer your energy to them. This will ensure that they begin to feel the same way you do.

Creating and playing music takes more energy than speaking. Emulating that experience can help you access extra energy to use when presenting. In fact, through visualisation, you can imagine how you feel in many situations to help create more and more energy for whatever it is you want to do.

For example, if I imagine running down a forest trail with a monster at my heels, my energy expenditure is sure to rise. This is one way to awaken your energy and passion prior to doing a presentation.

| Staying Small |

Mary Morrissey shared the following story as part of her Dream Builder coaching course in 2012.

There was a young guy who hears about this great fishing stream. He goes to the fishing stream and he throws in his line and he waits. Meanwhile he happens to notice that a little ways down the bank is an elderly fisherman. He's throwing in his line and this guy is just pulling in one fish after another. And every fish he pulls out of the stream, he takes it and he lays it down on the edge of the riverbank and he measures it against a broken-off ruler that's on the edge of the bank. If the fish is bigger than the broken-off ruler, he unhooks the fish and he tosses it back in the stream. If, however, the fish is smaller than the broken off ruler, he unhooks it and he puts it in his bucket. So the young guy is thinking, why is he doing that? Why is he unhooking the big fish and throwing them back, and unhooking the little fish and keeping them?

He finally just can't stand it, and he goes down and interrupts the old guy. He says, "Excuse me but, why are you throwing the big fish back and keeping the little ones? Do they get bony if they get big or is there some ordinance about taking the big fish out of the stream?" The old guy looks at him and says "Sonny, look at this. I measure every fish by that brokenoff ruler. See that broken-off ruler right there?" And the younger man says "yes," and he says "I measure every fish by that broken-off ruler because that broken-off ruler is broken off at exactly the size of the frying pan I use."

We laugh at a fisherman who did that, right? But unconsciously you and I do the same thing. The stream of life tosses us a big dream, a big fish, and we measure it by the frying pan we've got. We say ooh, it's not going to fit in this pocket. I don't have the money, I don't have the education. I don't have the context. My current conditions don't predict my ability to make use of that big idea. So we toss it back to the stream of life and say give me a fish—an idea—that fits. Now you've just gotten hold of a big fish here. You talked about it, you brought it to mind. You described it—your big fish—it's out there.

CHAPTER 2
THE 4 Ps OF POWERFUL PRESENTERS

| **Chapter 2 -** The 4 Ps of Powerful Presenters |

In the Introduction, I promised to help turn you into a powerful presenter. This chapter introduces the four essential tools that will move your presentation skills to the next level and beyond. I call them the "4 Ps of Powerful Presenters." Subsequent chapters will provide more detail on each; however, let's first get a feel for what they are and why they work so powerfully together.

| **Purpose** |

Every successful speaker has a purpose for their presentation. They understand who the audience is, and they have a core message to impart. They also know the action they want their audience to take.

It is common for presenters to be self-focused. They have a lot to say and often very little time to prepare. Think of yourself. You want to give the best presentation possible. However, these constraints make it hard to do so. They may even make you nervous. In such a high-pressure situation it is easy to forget what is really important—and that is the audience. If you become so consumed by your performance or overly focused on pushing through your core message that you forget the audience is even there, you can miss cues from them or misjudge their needs. This classic story from Chief Executive Officer (CEO) Coach Tony Jeary illustrates how not knowing your audience can completely ruin your presentation.

Many years ago a local television news anchorman visited a local high school in suburban New York. He was there to speak to an auditorium full of seniors nearing graduation. The anchorman was the top gun at a major market affiliate. The students eagerly awaited his visit. The media aid was not yet in full blossom. The world of 500 television channels had just begun.

Neither the internet or cell phones existed in public awareness, nor did everyone get to be famous for 15 minutes. So a guy who many students saw on the television every night and now visiting in the flesh had a chance to make a real impression on these students.

They sat at first, in rapt attention as the anchorman launched into a story culled from his vast experience as a reporter. It was a sort of shaggy dog story, one of those that goes on and on. Some of the students started checking their watches when the story had lasted 10 minutes and showed no sign of let up! After a while the 400 or so students began to stir. 15 minutes passed and the story was still going. Fifteen minutes is like a lifetime to a bored 18-year-old. Yet the anchorman droned on. Twenty minutes. A steady murmur began to work its way through the audience. They had started to fidget, then to whisper to their friends. Soon many of the students were speaking to one another at half volume. The speaker stopped and peered into the crowd, but the students didn't even notice. The anchorman had to call for quiet, but the calls were largely ignored. This lack of response rattled him visibly. Those in the nearer rows could see that his face had gone red. He pleaded for quiet again and again in increasingly strident tones and then tried to go on with his remarks, but by this time he had completely lost his audience. Half an hour earlier than planned, the anchorman brought his speech to an abrupt and uneasy conclusion.

| Misusing Your Inner Energy |

The true story above also illustrates how a speech can go awry when the speaker makes it all "about him." This TV personality's second big mistake was to assume that his own famous face and voice was so compelling that it would override any other considerations

I attended a presentation a few weeks ago. It was well-crafted overall, and the presenter was well-established in his industry. However, he did not do a thorough analysis of the demographics of his audience before crafting the last section of the two-day event.

He was selling a high priced package without realising that most of the attendees were unable to afford it. As a result, not only did he lose the audience, but a handful of people left the room quite upset.

As a presenter, you are in the front of the room and have the attention of an audience that is ready to hear you speak. It is a given. This makes it too easy to feel as if you are in a position of power which, of course, is a dangerous view to hold. Why? The reality is that the audience is the star of the show. They are the ones who determine if your idea, product or information lives or dies. They have the power of choice: the power to embrace or reject what you are trying to offer them. You have to be aware of this and carefully understand your audience's needs. Be conversational in your approach and create a passionate presentation that resonates with them and their needs.

Identifying and understanding the audience has to be your first priority. Who are they? What are they like? What issues do you know or believe they struggle with? How do you want them to change as a result of your presentation? Why and how will your message make them more successful?

Now you are ready to build a powerful presentation that will win over your audience right away.

| Passion |

The fire inside you... topics that set your heart to racing, absorb you and possess you.

Communication always comes down to passion and inner energy. You cannot inspire anyone else unless you are truly inspired yourself. For example, if Steve Jobs had not pursued his passion for music he may never have created an MP3 player that fits in our pockets today.

If he had not pursued his passion for animation, millions of children—and adults — may never have experienced the joy of watching Toy Story, Finding Nemo and Cars. The list goes on—the iPhone, the iPad—these were all the results of one man who followed his heart.

Howard Schultz, the founder of Starbucks, is not as passionate about coffee so much as he is passionate about building a third place between work and home, a place where employees are treated with respect and offer exceptional customer service. Coffee is the product, but Starbucks is in the business of customer service.

You need to find out what inspires you—the thing that ignites your inner fire, giving you the energy and inward passion that will allow your heart to sing.

Asking yourself, "What's my product or service?" is not nearly as effective as asking yourself, "What business am I really in? In other words, what am I truly passionate about?"

Becoming a speaker who is energetic, enthusiastic, and passionate increases the odds that you will establish a connection with your audience.

What are you truly passionate about? Make your response an instant one, rather than a long, drawn out answer or a list. And, once you find or discover this passion of yours, ask yourself the deeper questions: What makes my heart sing? Can I incorporate what makes my heart sing into what I do professionally?

| Preparation |

Practise, practise, practise.

Nothing can help your presentation skills more than simply practising what you have to say over and over and over again, working on every nuance and gesture, focusing on your delivery – that is, on how your voice resonates and how you speak, fast or slow, projecting or not, the stance you take and even your warm up exercises. When you do these things, you are not simply memorising; you are creating what is called "muscle memory."

The term muscle memory or motor learning is a form of procedural memory that involves bringing "a specific motor task into memory through repetition."[2] As a movement, or a set of movements, is repeated over time, a long-term muscle memory is created for that task, eventually allowing it to be performed without conscious effort. This process decreases the need for attention and creates maximum efficiency within the motor and memory systems. Examples of muscle memory are found in many everyday activities that become automatic and improve with practice, such as riding a bicycle, typing on a keyboard,[3] typing in a PIN number, playing a musical instrument, or martial arts.

[2] https://en.wikipedia.org/wiki/Muscle_memory.

[3] https://en.wikipedia.org/wiki/Outline_of_the_human_brain.

| Presentation |

Trusting your mind.

Throughout my teaching career, I have noticed many potential speakers freeze with fear and pain. When I help those people ease their fear and discomfort, it is like starting a new life, all through learning how to communicate.

It is almost funny how easily we can get scattered, especially when presenting. So many things call for our attention that we may even forget where we are in our speech or keep our eyes on the slides rather than on the audience. Survey results indicate that:

- *60% of presenters admitted to using their slides to help remember what to say with little or no eye contact. They also admitted to being frequently nervous prior to presentations. Only one-third of the people surveyed felt that they were influential, persuasive presenters and 75% "believed that they would gain more respect for their knowledge and expertise in the business world if they were better public speakers."* [4]

- *More than one-half of audience participants said that presenters generally read from their slides. Only 38% of respondents thought presenters understood their needs, and fewer than 29% of those surveyed said that they were moved to take action.*

How do you keep yourself grounded and focused on your core message and the audience at the same time? Reconnecting with your body is the fastest way to achieve a peaceful, powerful presence. One of the most effective things you can do when trying to improve any skill is to visualise. It works for Olympic athletes, and it can work for you.

When you follow and use the 4 Ps, you will be ready and able to communicate in a powerful and persuasive way. You will remember that the audience is your purpose, and you will have done your homework so that you understand the people in that audience and know what they need. Having been released from your fear, you will be able to harness your passion for what you are presenting, thereby capturing the attention of your audience, and instilling them with a passion for your core message. And, finally, with proper preparation and practice, your presentation will go smoothly and allow for better interaction with those listening.

Good presentations are not the norm. Giving a powerful presentation will make you stand out in the right way. The 4 Ps help you do just that.

[4] Why Presentation Skills Are So Important For Career Success, http://businessblueprint.com.au/team-building/presentation-skills-for-career-suc (accessed February 22, 2017).

CHAPTER 3
PURPOSE

| **Chapter 3** - Purpose |

As a presenter, it is critical you understand that the audience does not need to fine-tune itself to you. Rather, you will want to tune your message to them. Your audience will only be inspired when you communicate an idea that caters to their needs and desires. When you understand the hearts and the minds of your audience, you will be able to resonate with them. You will then be able to generate a powerful response and create change.

Your first essential tool for becoming a powerful presenter, therefore, is **Purpose** which, as you read in the previous chapter, involves finding your core message (the Big Idea) and understanding your audience and what motivates them so you can get them to accept, adopt, and implement your Big Idea. This initial step requires that you dig deep, do your homework and relate to your audience.

When you have considered what you want to say, do not write it out or say it, until you know the words that will inspire your audience to say "yes."

| **Know Your Audience** |

Nancy Duarte, a famous TED speaker, was preparing to present to executives at a beer manufacturer. She does not like beer and was totally unfamiliar with the industry. She started her research by reading the company's annual report and checking out recent press. She also studied the key influencers and did an online search of every person who was scheduled to attend her presentation. Duarte then went a step further and hosted a beer tasting event at her office to determine how her staff felt about the company and its products. Because of all her background preparation, she was able to answer a question posed by one of the top executives by citing relative examples.

Knowing the names and titles of the people who will be attending your presentation is a great first step. However, powerful presenters also find out what their audience needs, and understands the challenges they face. In that way, the presenter can craft their presentation to show how the core message is the solution to the audience's concerns and problems.

A self-centred presenter may announce a new project, explain what needs to get done, outline how to do it when to do it, and the budget required to get it done—and maybe if the audience is lucky, they will have a slide at the end to outline Why It Even Matters! A powerful presenter, on the other hand, spends a minute in their audience's shoes. They let people know why the initiative matters to them, the audience. A powerful presenter also explains or reviews the internal and external factors driving the project and why the audience's support is going to make it successful. When you present, let your audience know about the valuable role they play in the scenario rather than dictating a laundry list of things they need to do.

| Know Them as Individuals |

If you look at your audience as a faceless bunch of strangers, you will not be able to establish a connection or move them to action. Rather, see them as a line-up of individuals that are waiting to have a conversation with you.

- What are they like as people?
- What is their relationship to each other?
- Who stands where in the decision-making hierarchy?

Your audience almost always consists of a variety of people: individuals from various roles and positions, different departments of an organisation, and different industries.

Each one needs to hear your message for different reasons. It is important to recognise which sub-group is the most significant and target their needs.

| Sharpen Your Focus |

When you focus on the audience, you will want to consider five critical factors:

1. **Power:** Includes power, influence, and the decision-making process.

2. **Demographics:** Addresses age, education, ethnicity, gender, and geography.

3. **Psychographics:** May include their personality, values, attitudes, interests, communities, and lifestyle.

4. **Firmographics:** Consists of a bit more practical information, such as the number of employees, the revenue size, industry, number of locations and location of the headquarters.

5. **Ethnographics:** Addresses the social and cultural needs your audience may have.

| Establish a Connection |

Knowing your audience members politically, demographically, and psychographically is a very good start; however, really connecting deeply with people means understanding them on a more personal level. To develop content that resonates with them dig deeper for insights about them. Find something interesting about them and resonate with them there. Ask yourself questions such as these[5]:

[5] Presenting Skills: Know your Presentation Audience | Duarte, http://www.duarte.com/presenting-skills-know-your-presentation-audience

- **What are they like?** *Think through a day in their lives. Outline what a typical day looks like for them to help you understand life from their perspective.*

- **Why are they here?** *What do they think they are going to get out of this presentation? Are they willing participants or mandatory attendees? Highlight what is in it for them.*

- **What keeps them up at night?** *Everyone has a fear or a pain point or a thorn in their side. Let your audience know that you empathise and that you are here to help them.*

- **How can you solve their problems?** *How are you going to help their lives get better? What benefits will they care about?*

- **What do you want them to do?** *What is your part in their plan? Make sure there is a clear action for your audience to take.*

- **How may they resist?** *What will keep them from adopting your message and carrying out your call to action? Remove any obstacles you can.*

- **How can you best reach them?** *How do they prefer to receive information? Do they want materials to review before the presentation or afterward? Do they like the room to be set up in a certain way? What atmosphere or type of media will best help them see your point of view? Give them what they want and how they want it.*[6]

[6] Ibid.

| Segment Your Audience |

It is important to segment your audience before you create your presentation so you can cater your message in a way that resonates with your audience. When you start to write your presentation, picture yourself as a curator of content for your most valuable and powerful stakeholders. While the presentation needs to also appeal to the broader group, tailor most of your specifics to the sub-group that you have targeted as the most important.

Let us imagine that you are about to recommend a major new product acquisition to the Board of Directors of a large corporation. This Board is made up of five very different executives with very different needs. John, the CEO, has been in his position for slightly less than a year, having been recruited from a competitor. He has a dominant personality and is anxious for his first "big win." Shannon is the President of the Consumer Division. She is a visionary and more creative than John, on whom she wants to make a good impression. Her buy-in is especially important as the acquisition will become her responsibility after its first two years with the company. First, however, it will be part of the Acquisitions and New Products Division, which is run by Peter, a Vice President who has been with the company for more than ten years. The other members of the Board often look to him for background and advice. And then there is Steve, the Chief Marketing Officer, who was brought over from the competitor by the CEO. He can often be arrogant and tends to sabotage projects that are not his own. Lastly, Greg is the Chief Technology Officer (CTO). He is political, analytical and risk-averse.

This segmentation analysis will be especially important to you when creating and practising your presentation. By knowing who the true decision-makers and influencers are, you can incorporate the facts each would need to help persuade them to say yes to what you are proposing. Of course, the CEO can buy in to your idea; however, also in play is how the people most immediately affected by the acquisition will vote (Steve, Peter, and Shannon).

You may first appeal to Peter's entrepreneurial nature by explaining how exciting the new market is and how much room there is to grow the overall business. You may also try to work with, and not against, Steve's ego by asking for his counsel on a key marketing point or two before the group meets. And, while keeping in mind what the other executives will care about, you are likely to present data, trends, and analytics to cater to Greg, the analytical and risk-averse CTO, and to Shannon, who needs to know the long-term potential of the product acquisition.

| Find Common Ground |

Another way to resonate with your audience is to find common ground that transcends business. Think about what interests or beliefs you share and use them to tap into something that is already inside of the members of your audience. All this may sound highly unscientific and touchy-feely; yet, as the best-selling author Dr. Robert Cialdini explains in Influence: *The Psychology of Persuasion*, people are much more likely to favour those who are similar to themselves.

Additionally, a recent study in *The Oxford Journal* discovered that during lower-quality presentations, the brain activity of audience members was out of sync. Conversely, throughout higher-quality speeches, listeners as a group were more coupled to each other. This suggests that effective presentations are more potent in taking control of the listeners' neural responses.

| Discover Similarities |

Perhaps you and the key decision-makers have mutual friends or acquaintances that are willing to share insights with you. There may be recent publications or posts on social media that can provide background information that includes their interests, hobbies, education and likes. Remember, even sharing a first name or owning the same type of dog can help establish common ground. Also, look to capitalize on:

- **Shared Experiences:** *What from your past do you have in common? Do you have shared memories, historical events or interests? Did you go to the same university, play the same type of sports, or belong to the same fraternity or sorority?*

- **Common Goals:** *Where are you all headed in the future? What types of outcomes are mutually desired?*

- ***Your Qualifications: :*** *Why are you uniquely qualified to be this audience's guiding expert? What did you learn when you faced similar challenges of your own? How will your audience benefit from that insight?*

| Be a Mentor and Coach |

Even though presentations and audiences vary, Duarte reminds us that one significant factor always remains constant: the people in the "audience came to see" what you can do for them, not what they can do for you. "See the audience as the hero of your idea" and yourself as the mentor who helps people get behind your idea and make it successful.

Duarte shares a wonderful example of this principle:

Yoda is a wise and humble mentor. In the Star Wars movies, he gives the hero, Luke Skywalker, a special gift, which was a deeper understanding of the forest, trains him to use a magical tool, which was the lightsaber, and he helps him in his fight against the Empire.

Just as Yoda and other mentors in myths and movies, presenters will want to do these three things:

1. **Give the hero a special gift!** In other words, you will want to give your audience insights that will improve their lives. You can introduce senior managers to an exciting way to compete in the marketplace or show potential clients how you can save them money and time.

2. **Teach the hero to use a magical tool.** This is where the people in your audience pick up a new skill or a new mindset from you – something that enables them to reach their objectives and yours.

3. **Help the audience get unstuck!** Ideally, you will come to the presentation with an idea or solution that gets the audience out of a difficult or a painful situation. For instance, if you are gearing

up to launch a new service offering, give your team the magical gift of a clear roadmap or the promise to bring in new consultants to provide training and support. Finally, you may help them get unstuck by describing how these new tools will help everyone rise to the challenge ahead."

| Engage in Conversation |

When your audience is familiar to you — let us say it is a group of your direct reports or your colleagues —think through the pressures they are under and find ways to create an empathetic connection. Knowing people, really knowing them, makes it easier to influence them. You are likely to engage in conversations, exchange insights and tell stories comfortably when you know someone well and, usually, you will both change a little bit in the process. (The same holds true once you have worked with a client for a long time and have had the chance to build a relationship.)

People do not fall asleep in conversations; however, they often do during presentations, and that is because many presentations do not feel conversational. Knowing your audience will help you feel warmly towards the people in the room and take on a more conversational tone as if you are speaking to a friend. When you speak sincerely to an audience, people will want to listen to your presentation and contribute to the success of your idea.

| Senior Executives are Special |

Senior executives, also known as C-Level Executives, are a difficult group to present to. They are exceptionally busy and have very little time to hear you out. Although that is true for many audiences, what sets executives apart is the need to make huge decisions based on accurate information that is delivered quickly.

Lengthy presentations with a big "reveal" at the end do not work for them. You have to get to the bottom line right away. Because executives want insights quickly, they often will not even let you finish what you are saying without interrupting you. This can be frustrating because you may have addressed all their questions in the next two or three slides.

When you present to a group of C-Level Executives, these five things will help them make decisions more easily:

1. **Get to the point.** Take less time than you were allocated. For example, if you were given 40 minutes, create your presentation within that time frame — then imagine your time slot was cut to five minutes. This will force you to be straightforward and deliver the points executives care about, like high-level findings, conclusions, recommendations, and your call to action. You want to hit those points clearly and simply before you dive into supporting data.

2. **Give them what they asked for.** In other words, stay on topic. They have invited you because they feel you can supply a missing piece of information; therefore, you will want to answer that specific request quickly and early in your presentation. For example, if they invited you to give an update about an investment opportunity for a new property development, DO that before you do anything else. For a new property development, address that issue before you move on to the rest of your presentation.

3. **Set expectations.** In the beginning, let the executives know how you have planned to structure your time slot. For example, you can say that you plan to spend the first five minutes of your 30 minutes presenting the summary and the remaining 25 minutes on discussion. Most executives can be patient for five minutes and let you present your main points well if they know they can ask questions soon after.

4. **Create executive summary slides.** Develop a clear, short overview of your key points and place it in a set of executive summary slides that stay at the front of your deck. Have the rest of your slides serve as an appendix. Follow a ten percent rule of thumb, which means that if your appendix is 50 slides, devote about five slides to your summary. "After you present the summary, let the group drive the conversation." Often, the Executives will want to go deeper on the points that will aid "their decision-making. You can quickly pull up any slide in the appendix that speaks to those points of interest to them." [7]

5. **Review and rehearse.** Before your presentation, you can run your slides by someone who has success getting ideas adopted at the Executive Level and who will serve as an honest coach. Is your message coming through clearly and quickly? Do your summary slides boil everything down into "skimmable" insights (Duarte)? Are you missing anything that your audience is likely to expect? Do you think this sounds like a lot of work? You are right. However, presenting to an Executive Team is a great honour, and it "can open tremendous doors for you. If you nail this presentation, people with a lot of influence will become strong advocates for your ideas". [8] Also, If there are to be one or two key decision-makers in your audience, practise focusing your eye contact accordingly.

[7] Presenting to Senior Executives | Duarte, http://www.duarte.com/presenting-to-senior-executives).

[8] Ibid.

| Demonstrate Leadership |

A speaker automatically has their audience's attention; the big deal is to keep it. You do this by projecting your energy onto the audience and being positive. A powerful leader also deals with mistakes effectively. Anyone can make a mistake, and every presentation can have a minor disruption (someone enters late, a phone rings, a glass of water spills).

If you make a mistake, do not panic! Remain calm and positive, and deal with it as if it was not a big thing (even if it was). When a disruption occurs, handle it the same way. Acknowledge what happened ("Glad you were able to join us," "Do you need to take that call?" etc.) and move on, reminding your audience where you were before the disruption.

A powerful leader also walks the proverbial mile in the audience's shoes. Explain why the initiative or recommendation matters to them and the organisation. Talk about the internal and external factors driving your core message, and why it is that their support is going to make it successful. Yes, you can get into the itty, bitty details. However, you will want to first set up the valuable role they play in the scenario rather than dictate a laundry list of things for them to do.

| Crafting Your Core Message |

Now that you have a clear idea of how to analyse, understand, and resonate with your audience, your next step is to take what you are passionate about, what makes your heart sing, and turn it into a *BIG IDEA* that resonates with your audience.

Your Big Idea

This is the one key message that you have to share with your audience. It is what convinces the audience to change course. Screenwriters call this a "controlling idea, " and that is exactly what it is. Your Big Idea has two components:

1. **Your point of view:** The Big Idea needs to express your perspective on a subject and not a generalisation like "Q4 Financials." Otherwise, why present? You may as well email your stakeholders a spreadsheet and be done with it.

2. **What is at stake:** You will always want to convey why the audience cares about your perspective. This will help people recognise why they need to participate or change something rather than continuing with the status quo.

One Key Sentence

Once you have your Big Idea (the thing you are passionate about) and know what information will back your idea up (information that your audience needs to hear and to agree with), you can craft and clarify a relevant and resonant core message that expresses your Big Idea in a complete sentence. It needs a subject, which is often a version of the word "you," that highlights the audience's role. It also needs a verb to convey action and elicit emotion.

Use Emotion

People are hardly strangers to emotional appeal, and it is proven to be an effective tactic in advertising and sales material; therefore, why are presentations NOT emotional? It is because being emotional is an uncomfortable style for presenters in general, and especially for analytical professionals. At work, most people think, "They are not paying me to feel, they are paying me to do." Of course, that is true. However, if you cannot motivate your team and employers to move forward, or convince your customers to buy, then you are in trouble.

Powerful presenters understand that expressing emotion is not all about the performance. The point is to evoke emotion, not just express it. Doing so is quite simple. It will take some work; however, you do not require any special knowledge to do it.

Do Not Sell a Product, Present an Idea

As entrepreneur and TED Talk expert Chris Anderson has explained, the best presenters propose an idea and allow the audience to adopt it through shared experiences and views of the world. "If communicated properly, (ideas) are capable of changing, forever, how someone thinks about the world, and shaping their actions both now and well into the future.

Ideas are the most powerful force shaping human culture." You will want to build your idea, piece by piece, out of concepts that your audience already understands. The language you want to use to weave together concepts your listeners already have in their minds is their language, and the terms and concepts you present need to be familiar to your audience. "Metaphors can play a crucial role in showing how the pieces (of your idea) fit together because they reveal the desired shape of the pattern, based on an idea that the listener already understands," says Anderson. In other words, start where your audience is.

Selling, on the other hand, does not give you the same creditability as presenting an idea. It may imply that the major beneficiary of the sale will be you, not the members of your audience, and that is the last thing you want.

| Focus on the Benefits to Your Audience |

This can be especially important when presenting to C-Level Executives, who may not care about the logistics, but will care more about how adopting your idea will benefit them and the company. Most presenters understand and articulate the difference between simply listing features and then turning them into benefits. However, can you see how important it is to take the extra step of identifying the emotional payoff for the client? Very few presenters take the extra step —and it is that extra step that sells any idea, product or service. People want to know what is in it for them, and that is the emotional payoff. No one does anything unless they can feel good about their decision or, at the very least, that decision will help them to escape some kind of pain.

The next time you have to present something, list the types of pain you will be helping your audience escape, and the types of pleasure you will be bringing to them.

CHAPTER 4
PASSION

| **Chapter 4** - Passion |

"Nothing is as important as passion. No matter what you want to do with your life, be passionate." — **Jon Bon Jovi**

Passion is the fire inside you that can ignite a room full of people to take action. It comes from focusing on the ideas and things that absorb you and set your heart racing. It is very difficult and nearly *impossible* to electrify an audience without feeling an intense, meaningful connection to the content of your presentation.

A powerful presenter is one who is passionate about his or her ideas and recommendations and can enthuse their audience so that they, too, become passionate about what they need to do. Sometimes we have to create the feeling inside ourselves; however, as American businesswoman, investor, author, and television personality Barbara Corcoran says, "You cannot fake passion."

| **Be Inspired** |

Communication always comes down to passion and inner energy. You cannot inspire anyone else unless you are truly inspired yourself. In *Talk Like TED*, Carmine Gallo writes about James Cameron's "insatiable" sense of curiosity.

If it hadn't been for Ballard's discovery of the Titanic, one of the most successful films of all time may never have been made. "Curiosity is the most important thing you own," Cameron told a TED audience in February 2010. "Imagination is a force that can actually manifest a reality."

It seems that exploring the oceans ignited Cameron's imagination from the age of 15 when he became certified as a diver. He explained that when he made Titanic, he pitched it to the studios as "Romeo and Juliet on a ship." Cameron, however, had an ulterior motive: to dive to the real wreck of Titanic.

"And that's why I made the movie. And that's the truth. Now, the studio didn't know that. But I convinced them. I said, "We're going to dive to the wreck. We're going to film it for real. We'll be using it in the opening of the film. It will be really important. It will be a great marketing hook." And I talked them into funding an expedition.

| Passion Builds Trust |

Passion is both authentic and charismatic. We do not fully trust people until we have seen them get emotional: angry, sad, or ecstatic, for example, because these moments allow us to get the measure of their values. That is how we size others up. "If we see someone giving a tongue-lashing to a sales clerk because the store is out of an item, we make one kind of judgment about that person. If we see someone else standing up to a bully, we make another kind of judgment." [9]

Being passionate is ultimately about allowing yourself to experience the emotion fully. Inhabit it, revel in it and soak it up. That way you will send a consistent message, not a mixed or confusing one, and you will come across as an authentic communicator.

[9] Why Is Passion Important In Public Speaking? - Forbes, http://www.forbes.com/sites/nickmorgan/2014/12/23/why-is-passion-important

| Have Passion for the Benefit, Not the Product |

Tony Hseih of Zappo Shoes is not as passionate about shoes as he is about delivering happiness to his customers and having happy staff. Shoes are his vehicle, but delivering good service and happy customers is the impetus for the result. The questions he asks himself are:

- How do I make my employees happy?

- How do I make my clients happy?

Asking yourself, "What's my product or service?" is not nearly as effective as asking yourself, "What business am I really in?" or "What do I want to do for or give to others?" In other words, "What am I truly passionate about?"

You will want your responses to these questions to be instant and to the heart of the matter rather than a long, drawn out answer or list. And, once you find or discover this passion of yours, ask yourself these two deeper questions:

1. What makes my heart sing?

2. Can I incorporate what makes my heart sing into what I do professionally?

| The Bigger the End Benefit, the Greater the Passion |

Aimee Mullins has 12 pairs of legs. Like most people, she was born with two. However, she had both her legs amputated below the knee before her first birthday, because of a medical condition. As Mullins grew up, she refused to accept the label most people gave her of "disabled." She empowered herself by deciding that prosthetic limbs could give her superpowers, and then worked with scientists, designers, and artists to tap into those superpowers. In doing so, Mullins redefined what it means to be disabled, and has inspired countless others. Her prosthetic limbs do things others can only dream about. Mullins broke three world records in track and field at the 1996 Paralympics, and became a fashion model, an actress, and one of the 50 Most Beautiful People in People Magazine.

In 2009 she gave a TED talk about prosthetic limbs and innovations in bionics, but her message was about so much more than just providing information about prosthetics. It was really about turning what others think of as a disability into a chance to re-invent yourself. In the YouTube video of her TED talk, you can see that her passion really lies in unleashing human potential —and that is what helps her win over the hearts of thousands of people.

Here is another example: Carmine Gallo, author of Talk like TED, describes a wonderful story in his book:

There was a CEO in the agribusiness community of California. He headed an association of strawberry growers, an important crop for the state. When he was asked, "What do you do?" he said, "I'm the CEO of the California Strawberry Commission." The next question was, "What are you passionate about?" and he answered, "I'm passionate about promoting California strawberries!" And here is the most interesting question out of all – "What makes your heart sing?" and surprisingly, he said "The American Dream. My parents were immigrants and worked in the fields. Eventually, they were able to buy an acre of land, and it grew from there. With strawberries, you don't need a lot of land and you don't need to own it; you can lease it. It's a stepping stone to The American Dream."

| People Buy When They Identify |

Martin Luther King was a legendary leader of the American Civil Rights Movement; however, the enormous amount of support he received was not based solely on his leadership or preaching qualities. King gained the support of thousands of people, not because he went around telling people what needed to change in America, but by sharing his beliefs and dreams with great passion. The speech he gave was, "I Have a Dream," not "I Have a Plan." And, people who believed in his cause took that dream and made it their own.

People do not buy what you do, they buy why you do it. That is the power of passion!

None of this is simply my opinion. It is all grounded in biology, specifically in the way the brain responds to outside stimuli. As you probably remember from secondary school science classes, the brain is divided into sections, some of which are responsible for our ability to think, what we think and our emotions. The neocortex, for example, is a part of the cerebral cortex and is involved in our higher functions such as sensory perception, the generation of motor commands, spatial reasoning, conscious thought and language. In other words, the neocortex is responsible for all of our rational and analytical thought (www.sciencedaily.com/terms/neocortex.htm), making it the part of the brain that can understand facts and be influenced by numbers, data, and logic.

The limbic part of our brain is responsible for all of our human behaviour. That includes our feelings, like trust and loyalty, and all decision-making. When you communicate with passion, you stimulate that part of the brain in the members of your audience. Their brains react to the power of positive emotion and that, in turn, affects their decision-making. That is why storytelling (which we will discuss in-depth in the next chapter), with its ability to evoke emotion, is such a powerful tool for presenters.

A strong, powerful presentation appeals to both parts of the brain by providing emotional and practical stimulation. As Steve Jobs said, in his last major public presentation, "It is the intersection of technology and liberal arts that makes our hearts sing."

| An Audience Cannot Be Fooled |

Investors, customers, and other stakeholders are "smart consumers." They know when a person is displaying genuine passion and when they are faking it. It is very difficult, and nearly impossible, to electrify an audience without feeling an intense, meaningful connection to the content of your presentation.

Some people are uncomfortable with showing emotions; others think they have to hold their emotions in check lest they are seen as unprofessional. However, when you are wide open in front of your audience, when they can see your emotions and feel what you feel, they will respond to your truthfulness and honesty by becoming invested in what you have to say.

| Show Your Passion |

The sincerity of emotion shows up in nonverbal conversation in a variety of ways. While the strong passions—anger, joy, excitement of various kinds—can all be signaled with energetic body movements, sometimes extreme stillness can be just as effective. Think of it as being similar to your voice in that the point is to establish a baseline and then vary that to exhibit emotions. [10]

[10] Why Is Passion Important In Public Speaking? - Forbes, http://www.forbes.com/ sites/nickmorgan/2014/12/23/why-is-passion-important-in-public-speaking.

I worked with a speaker who was telling a personal story to a large audience and revealing information that had not been public before. There was a lot of tension within his staff before the big night. After talking with the speaker and suggesting different ways in which he may indicate his passion to that audience, simplicity seemed the best strategy. The result was he stood very still, told his story in a quiet manner, and the passion was very powerful and authentic.

That said, for most of us, when we want to telegraph passion, we do so with a raised or higher voice, and add more hand and arm gestures, as well as more body movement in general — all of which are signs of energy and passion that people are used to recognising.

Rather than thinking about this as a technical exercise, focus on the passion itself. Before you go into an important meeting, begin a high-stakes speech, or have that conversation with your teenager that you have been putting off, focus on the way you feel about the topic and the person or people with whom you are communicating.

Doing so has two benefits. Firstly, "it will put you in the moment if you do it well, allowing you to connect the two conversations (content and body language) and appear authentic and charismatic." Secondly, "it will occupy your mind and keep you from getting nervous. If you think only about your nerves, your self-consciousness, and how poorly the scene is certain to go, you will almost certainly telegraph nervousness" through your body language, and undercut your own best efforts.

Spend a moment outside the room before the meeting begins, and feel the excitement you have for the concept or recommendation you are about to propose, or the passion you feel for the company and where it is "headed, or the love you feel for your teenager who has to understand the importance of a curfew and personal safety."

| Generate Passion Even When You Do Not Feel It |

Not every presentation you give will be specifically about your Big Idea; however, you can bring the passion you have for your core message to every opportunity you have to present. Every step along the way is a chance to move your Big Idea ahead so, whether you are sharing schedules and new job descriptions with your staff, recapping activities for colleagues from other another department or sharing research results with a client, keep the end goal in mind. When you are positive and upbeat with even the everyday details, your audience will be enthused to move ahead, take on new responsibilities or go the proverbial extra mile.

Many presenters lack confidence or suffer from what actors call stage fright. If that is the case with you, passion can cure you in the most amazing ways. Here is one of the best examples I know of the transformative powers of being a passionate presenter:

The late Dr. Leo Buscaglia, a best-selling author, called Dr. Love by almost everyone who ever met him, dedicated most of his life to understanding what love is and how we can all embrace it in our relationships. He once spoke before an audience of several hundred people at USC. Buscaglia suffered from extreme presentation anxiety. When he came out on stage in a ratty old sweater, he jittered and jived, shook and scratched, and stuttered so badly that it was painful to watch; I could not believe it. I was caught up in what was going on as surely as if Les Brown, Zig Ziglar or Tony Robbins had walked out on stage.

Then something amazing happened: Buscaglia seemed to reach within himself and grab hold of the topic he was speaking about, the varied forms of love. And with this topic, one he spoke about in an open and vulnerable way, came passion. He threw his sweater off behind him on the stage, took hold of that audience and held on to them for the rest of his hour-long presentation. He mesmerized us and took us to an envisioned world filled with loving, caring people. Such was the effect of his emotional exposition that the audience became quiet, hardly breathing and unable to take their focus off the mousy little man who had turned into some kind of mystical giant.

And, when it was all over, the audience just sat there, stunned. You could have heard the proverbial pin drop.

Then, another amazing thing happened. Dr. Buscaglia offered a warm, heartfelt hug to anyone who wanted one. The audience got up as if waking from a dream and began to line up, the trail eventually leading out of the auditorium to God knows where. I found it hard to believe what I was seeing. It literally sent shivers down my spine.

| How to Summon Passion |

As cited in the Forbes article, "[11]great actors have something they call the offstage beat that they use just before they go onstage. Mediocre actors just walk on and deliver their first lines." However, the great ones begin inhabiting the character beforehand. They figure out where the character just came from and what state of mind they were in, and play that rather than simply "an actor coming on stage."The result is a fully believable character, one you cannot take your eyes off of.

As Olivia Schofield so aptly put, "An actor is an expert in being someone else. A speaker is an expert in being themselves." As such, you will want to develop a little of the same magic an actor uses. The way to do that is to prepare immediately before the presentation. Know what you are going to say and how you feel about it: strongly, fully, and with all your physical being. That, after all, is where passion originates. And that is how you radiate passion, align the two conversations (again, content and body language), and convince audiences large and small of your authenticity.

[11] How to Communicate with Passion - Public Words, http://www.publicwords.com/2014/12/23/how-to-communicate-with-passion.

I never forget—and you need to never forget— that if you do it (whatever it is) with enough conviction, you will be charismatic.[12]

In sum, passion is essential to captivating your audience. It can also be a driving force for overcoming your fears. If you visualise and meditate before your presentation, you will be able to articulate your core message with conviction; your passion will show, and you will be successful, even under fire.

[12] http://www.buscaglia.com/biography.aspx

CHAPTER 5
STORYTELLING
PRINCIPLES

| **Chapter 5** - Storytelling Principles |

A story told successfully is a little miracle – people see the world differently afterward.

Stories bring your presentation to life. When we hear them, our hearts race, our eyes dilate, we feel chills, we laugh, we clap, we lean forward, and we jump back. These actions are mostly involuntary because they are grounded in emotion, and evoking emotion among the members of your audience makes a huge difference in how your presentation is received.

Stories have the power to win customers, align colleagues, and motivate employees by adding emotional texture to a logical case that you have already built with your data, case studies, and other supporting evidence. In fact, stories are the most persuasive platform we have for managing imaginations, evoking emotions, and building rapport with your audience. Perhaps that is why we use them in 65% of all our communications with other people.

Additionally, stories are powerful tools that provide insights and demonstrate how beneficial it will be to adopt the beliefs and behaviours you are proposing in your presentation. Stories also help members of your audience make the transition from their current perspective to your world of ideas. That is why, when describing what can be, you will want to tell a story that strikes a little awe or fear in their hearts – something that inspires them to change!

At 29 years of age, former fashion model Renee Airya found the right part of her face paralised after massive brain surgery. She has given many speeches on the subject of "Flips and Flaws;" and, in one of those talks she included the following story:

I want to share a quick story to help flip that ugly definition of flaws being defects or blemishes. Some of you may know this story. When the ancient Greeks used to make pottery, many of the pieces came out flawed with cracks and blemishes. Naturally, the sellers wanted to hide these because they thought no one would want to buy these pieces. However, when the buyers would come in to purchase, they were willing to pay more for the pieces with the visible cracks and flaws because they saw them as being authentic and real. Did you know that the word "sincere" actually stems from the Latin word for insincerae? Meaning without wax.

Airya followed up her story by saying:

Maybe you can see what I am getting at here. Could it be possible that if we look at flaws through that lens of perception, flaws are actually gateways to our sincerity? In order to be a superhero, we do not need to gain some other power, but rather recover where we have been losing our power within ourselves. Could it be possible that flaws are actually a key to unlocking our uniqueness?

Personal stories told with conviction are by far the strongest tool in your arsenal, as audiences feel more inspired and affectionate towards speakers who reveal their own challenges and vulnerability through stories. Second and third-party stories are also powerful.

The key to delivering presentations that instantly inspire your audience is telling captivating stories in the first two to five minutes.

| Why the Story Form is So Powerful |

There is a simple scientific explanation for why the story form keeps people interested and attentive to what you are saying. Evolution has hardwired our brains for storytelling. When you watch and listen to any PowerPoint presentation, the language processing parts of your brain (the Broca and Wernicke areas) get activated, even if the presentation is a boring one.

This allows the audience to decode the sounds made into words. They can understand what you are saying and relate to your thoughts, based on their own experiences and knowledge. However, nothing happens in their brains to help them accept or relate warmly to what is said.

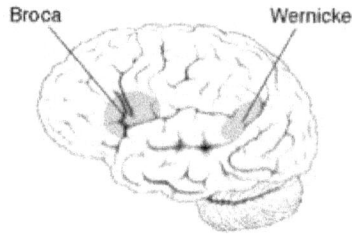

Source:
http://upload.wikimedia.org/wikipedia/commons/0/03/BrocasAreaSmall.png

On the other hand, when you tell stories you are sharing all sorts of details, such as what you saw, what you said, what you heard, what you tasted, what you smelled, and how you felt. By providing all these details, you evoke memories, associations, and feelings that activate more parts of your audience's brains and that, in turn, makes them more engaged in what you are saying.

| Be Engaging |

You will want to prepare your words and actions in story form as much as possible to keep your audience engaged all the way through your speech. Here are three examples of stimulating stories with clear, engaging messages:

The Girl Who Drew God

In 2006, Sir Ken Robinson stood on the TED Stage to present an astounding concept to cultivate creativity and acknowledge multiple types of intelligence in the traditional school systems. Instead of elaborating on diminutive details, he illustrated his ideas beautifully with the following story:

I heard a great story recently. I love telling it — of a little girl who was in a drawing lesson. She was six, and she was at the back, drawing. The teacher said this girl hardly ever paid attention, and in this drawing lesson, she did. The teacher was fascinated. She went over to her, and she asked, "What are you drawing?" And the girl said, "I'm drawing a picture of God." And the teacher said, "But nobody knows what God looks like." And the girl said, "They will, in a minute."

Needless to say, Robinson won the hearts of the audience within the first five minutes, and is considered one of the best TED speakers.

A Promise to Mama

In 2012, Bryan Stevenson, a renowned attorney and Law professor, delivered a TED talk about the importance of identity. Before presenting the inconceivable statistics regarding crime and injustice in the United States, he began the presentation with a story:

I grew up in a house that was the traditional African-American home that was dominated by a matriarch, and that matriarch was my grandmother. She was tough, she was strong, and she was powerful. She was the daughter of people who were actually enslaved. Her parents were born in slavery in Virginia in the 1840's. She was born in the 1880's and the experience of slavery very much shaped the way she saw the world.

One day, she took me out back, and she said, "Bryan, I'm going to tell you something, but you don't tell anybody what I tell you. I want you to know I've been watching you." And she said, "I think you are special." She said, "I think you can do anything you want to do." I will never forget it.

And then she said, "I just need you to promise me three things, Bryan." I said, "Okay, Grandma." She said, "The first thing I want you to promise me is that you'll always love your mom." She said, "That's my baby girl, and you have to promise me now you'll always take care of her."

Well, I adored my mom, so I said, "Yes, Grandma. I'll do that." Then she said, "The second thing I want you to promise me is that you'll always do the right thing even when the right thing is the hard thing." And I thought about it, and I said, "Yes, Grandma. I'll do that." Then finally she said, "The third thing I want you to promise me is that you'll never drink alcohol." Well, I was nine years old, so I said, "Yes, Grandma. I'll do that."

When I was about 14 or 15, one day my brother came home, and he had this six-pack of beer. I don't know where he got it, but he grabbed me and my sister, and we went out in the woods. He had a sip of this beer, and he gave some to my sister, and she had some, and they offered it to me. I said, "No, no, no. That's okay. You all go ahead. I'm not going to have any beer." My brother said, "Come on. We're doing this today; you always do what we do. I had some, your sister had some. Have some beer." I said, "No, I don't feel right about that. Y'all go ahead. Y'all go ahead." And then my brother started staring at me. He said, "What's wrong with you? Have some beer." Then he looked at me real hard, and he said, "Oh, I hope you are not still hung up on that conversation Grandma had with you." I said, "Well, what are you talking about?" He said, "Oh, Grandma tells all the grandkids that they're special." I was devastated.

And I'm going to admit something to you. I'm going to tell you something I probably shouldn't. I know this may be broadcast broadly. But I'm 52 years old, and I'm going to admit to you that I've never had a drop of alcohol. I don't say that because I think that's virtuous; I say that because there is power in identity. When we create the right kind of identity, we can say things to the world around us that (we) do not actually believe (or that) makes sense. We can get them to do things that they don't think they can do. When I thought about my grandmother, of course she would think all her grandkids were special. My grandfather was in prison during prohibition. My male uncles died of alcohol-related diseases. And these were the things she thought we needed to commit to.

Stevenson was able to resonate with the audience because he successfully conveyed the power of identity through a heartfelt story. In fact, his talk was so victorious that the audience donated a combined total of $1 million to his non-profit organisation.

A Crowded Vegas Convention

Ford president and CEO, Mark Fields, delivered his first keynote at the Consumer Electronics Show (CES) as the new head of the company in 2015. Fields began the presentation by establishing a theme: Ford is passionate about designing products to address very serious problems in major cities around the world, such as population density and congestion.

Who finds it easy to get around Las Vegas during the show? Fields asked as the audience laughed at the obvious reference to the notorious crowds during the CES week.

It really is a challenge to get around Vegas during the show. But think about this. The Las Vegas metro area has just more than one million people. And with a population density of roughly 1,750 people per square kilometer, it puts Las Vegas at number 120 on the list of the largest cities in the world by population density. During CES, there's an influx of another 150,000 people, most of them are concentrated right here on the strip. We put up with this for a few days. Imagine what people in Mumbai, India, face every day. More than 18 million people live in Mumbai, and its population density is 17 times greater than here in Las Vegas.

By building the comparison between something familiar, a crowded Vegas convention, and something unfamiliar to most of the audience—Mumbai congestion — Fields created an unforgettable story that framed the rest of the discussion to show how Ford can tackle the problem of population density.

| Have a Clear Structure |

Good stories and good presentations in general often convey and resolve a conflict or imbalance. The sense of friction that the problem/ solution structure conjures up is what makes audiences care enough to get and stay on board. As Nancy Duarte has explained extremely well, some of the best speeches and presentations of all time — such as those of Martin Luther King Jr. and Steve Jobs — create conflict and contrast by juxtaposing the present situation with a potential future. That is, "they alternately build tension and provide release by toggling back and forth between the status quo and a better way, finally arriving at the New Future people will discover by adopting the proposed beliefs and behaviours."

That persuasive structure happens within the basic beginning, middle and end storytelling structure, also known as a narrative. If you only have your audience for a short period of time (as is often the case with executives), the narrative will get your point across; however, fleshing out your story with physical action, sensations and internalised thoughts can bring your audience further into your story. You may also find it helpful to include an emotional arc that shows how the hero of your story (be it an animal, a person or even a product) transitions from one mood, attitude or belief to another. (In the following chapter you will see how to use this structure in creating presentations.)

| The Seven Step Anecdote Pattern |

Stories told for business purposes differ from stories told in other contexts. Unlike a "shaggy dog" story you may share with friends at a party, a story told in a work situation — on a job interview, during a presentation, while schmoozing with potential clients — arrives at a clear, concise and inspiring message.

The very first thing you will want to do is to figure out how the story will end. Ask yourself: What point do I mean to prove? What moral do I want my incidents to illustrate? What motto do I want ringing in their heads, calling them to action for weeks or months afterward? It is important you get the wording of that final thought just right. You are likely to end up revising your story over time until you are completely happy with its telling.

1. Start with the point you want to make.

2. Then explain when, who, where.

3. Add context.

4. Explain the conflict.

5. Propose a resolution.

6. Create a complication.

7. Provide the actual resolution.

One of the grand classics of storytelling for business is the Townsend[13] translation of the original text of Aesop's "The Hare and the Tortoise."

[13] Reverend George Fyler Townsend translated the standard English edition of Aesop's Fables in the 1800s.

A Hare one day ridiculed the short feet and slow pace of the Tortoise, who replied, laughing: "Though you be swift as the wind, I will beat you in a race." The Hare, believing her assertion to be simply impossible, assented to the proposal; and they agreed that the Fox should choose the course and fix the goal. On the day appointed for the race, the two started together. The Tortoise never for a moment stopped but went on with a slow but steady pace straight to the end of the course. The Hare, lying down by the wayside, fell fast asleep. At last waking up, and moving as fast as he could, he saw the Tortoise had reached the goal and was comfortably dozing after her fatigue. Slow but steady wins the race.

That is probably not the version of the story you know. Most of Aesop's Fables have been jazzed up and loaded with new details in modern adaptations. You too can tell stories in bare bones form like Aesop did, or in more expansive, fleshed-out ways like the famous Walt Disney animated short of that story. It depends on how much time you have, who is in your audience, and which version will resonate with them best. And yes, you can use fictional and even unrealistic stories in business situations. You may bore people with this particular story by Aesop because it is well known; people prefer to be surprised by stories if possible.

There is, however, a point for my using this particular story here, and that is the story has a point! No matter what version you read or see on film, this story always ends with its Controlling Idea, "Slow and steady wins the race." It is pithy, it is concise, and it is encouraging. But most importantly, it clearly asserts what was proven by the incidents described.

| Curating Stories |

Stories are so important to your presentation that you will want to choose them before you start the actual creation of PowerPoint slides. Think about the overall points you want to convey during your speech, and find an appropriate story that illustrates the idea. They can come from your work history or personal life. The story you choose and the point you want to make will be intertwined. As such, once you match the two together you may find you have to tweak the wording of the point you want to make. Or, you may find you have to re-direct the main emphasis of the story you have chosen. It is perfectly alright to tweak either the point or the story during the preparation and practice stages or while preparing your presentation.

| Create a Special Moment |

One of the most powerful things you can do is create a memorable moment in your presentation that will drive your Big Idea home and register so strongly with your audience that people will talk about it afterwards. You will want the audience to connect with it emotionally as well as intellectually. There are many ways to give your audience such a moment; here are five such tools that are used quite often by skilled presenters.

Dramatic Demonstration

Bill Gates effectively used this technique during a TED talk several years ago. He was speaking about the dangers of malaria when he opened a jar of what he said were infected mosquitoes, releasing them into the audience. The attendees were notably shaken by this dramatic gesture that brought the problem home to the audience in a striking and highly attention-getting manner. Although Gates immediately explained "I was just having you on," that did not dilute the power of his demonstration.

Repeatable Slogan

Great political and motivational speakers employ short, pithy statements which are repeated throughout their presentation, often for emphasis or to energise their audience. The slogans are easy to remember and short enough to be reposted via social media or included as a "sound bite" in the media. You may find this a particularly useful tool for energising a large audience or as a rallying cry for employees.

Arresting, Provocative Images

Compelling visuals evoke emotions and grab your audience's attention. They are easily recalled afterwards and are likely to re-evoke the same sense of excitement or emotion.

Startling Statistics

Numbers speak for themselves, especially when what they are saying is shocking or highly unexpected.

Emotional Anecdotes and Metaphors

Making a comparison that hits home with the people at your presentation can help draw a memorable picture in the minds of your audience and help attach a relatable emotion or thought to your idea. Metaphors are also useful devices for explaining a difficult or novel idea and make the unfamiliar familiar. Martin Luther King's "I Have a Dream" speech is a powerful and moving example of how to use metaphors.

CHAPTER 6
PREPARATION
PART ONE

| **Chapter 6 -** Preparation Part One |

Natural-born presenters who can successfully speak to an audience off-the-cuff are very rare. Almost all of us have to prepare and practise in terms of the language we will use, the tone and timbre of our voice, and our body language. Good speech habits such as enunciating properly and varying your pitch will bring emphasis and clarity to your speech. Deliberate gestures and purposeful movements linked to your message will bring power to your presentations. All of this will come from preparation and practice, as will a strong, healthy dose of self-confidence that can ease your fears and make you a stand-out presenter.

| **Organising Your Presentation** |

Once you have your core message and supporting points, as well as the key stories you want to include, you will be ready to prepare your presentation. Your first step will be to organise your information and conclusion in a logical and cohesive manner. As you read in the previous chapter, powerful presentations have a distinct beginning, middle, and end structure, customised based on what your audience needs and wants to hear.

Start at the Beginning

Begin your presentation by describing the current situation, and your audience will be nodding their heads in recognition because you will be explaining what they already understand to be true. This will create a bond between you and them, and it will make them more likely to listen to your ideas. After you have set the baseline of what is, introduce your idea of what can be. The gap between the two (what is and what can be) is going to throw your audience off balance, and that is a good thing because it creates a tension that needs to be resolved.

Make a Persuasive Argument for Change

At this point, you will be entering the most compelling part of your presentation. As touched on in the previous chapter, you will want to create a bridge between what is and what can be, most probably by contrasting between the two scenarios, moving back and forth between them as a structural device. As you do, the audience will suddenly start to find the former unappealing, and the latter, alluring.

For example, let's assume that revenues for your company are down and you have to motivate the employees to make up for the loss. You may choose to start your presentation by stating the facts, that is the situation as it exists: sales are down versus last year by 20%. You may then lay out a scenario in which sales do not increase and, therefore, the company does not give out end-of-the-year bonuses. You can then give your audience an alternate version of the future, in which your sales numbers improve substantially, and bonuses are forthcoming.

Then, segue into a review of the reasons why sales are down, alternating between various problems and their potential solutions. For example, perhaps your company will gain more manufacturing projects by updating the factory, bringing in new and updated equipment. To do so, you may recommend bringing in experts from another company to help install the new equipment and train the staff. You can also suggest a new marketing program to help in the acquiring of at least ten new clients next year.

Close With a Strong Call to Action

Many presentations end with a list of action items. That is not really inspiring. The end of your presentation needs to leave people with a heightened sense of what can be, and the willingness to believe in and do something new. You want people to feel ready to right the wrong and conquer the problem.

By skillfully defining the New Future and its rewards, you will be able to compel people to get on board with your ideas. Show them that taking action will be worth their effort.

This creates a vision of how their world can be when they adopt your ideas. In this example, you may start to close with something such as, "We have the opportunity to turn this company around and make things better and easier for all of us. If we all pitch in we can make the new sales goals and get our full bonuses, as well as a few days off over the holidays."

| Create the Right Balance |

Once you have the structure for your presentation, you will be ready to create your individual slides. Use a mix of words, figures and, more importantly, visuals to keep your audience attentive. Pictures are especially important at the beginning of your presentation to grab your audience's attention and to set the right emotional stage for the rest of your presentation. You will also want to limit the words you use per slide to keep your presentation moving. And, do not shy away from statistics; use them to shock your audience out of their comfort zone.

 After your slides have been created, you will then want to step back and review them, not merely to confirm that they are clear and concise, but also to see if you have the right mix of emotional and analytical content. If you feel you need to make your proposal stronger, look at the evidence and present it in a more impactful way.

To make a more emotional impact, you can add it by including more stories. Perhaps your presentation is technical in nature, in which case you may be thinking, "How do I tell a personal story when I am presenting statistics, data, and technology?" A story told by Symantec Cloud Group President Rowan Trollope in May 2012 is a wonderful example of how this can work. It is a gripping personal story that presents information of a technical nature:

I went mountain climbing with two of my friends to Mount Laurel in the Eastern Sierras. I am not a very experienced climber. However, my friends were even less experienced. We had been climbing for about 19 hours, and we were up 11,000 feet, and it was getting dark quite fast.

We needed to get down the side of this mountain... and we needed to do it quickly. Descending first, I got to a ledge and started to get our line ready. Climbers carry two emergency pitons with them for just this purpose. I'd never used them before, but I knew how they worked.

I took out my hammer and started hammering one of the pitons into the rock. The books tell us that you'll hear the tone of the hammer strike change when it is "IN" the rock. I heard a loud ping with each strike of the hammer and decided it was in "GOOD ENOUGH."

The books also tell you, though, to always use two pitons. So I used both of the pitons that I had with me. As I hammered the second one into the rock, I heard a sharp, high-pitched ping at the end. I tied the knots and got our line ready. By this time, my buddies had reached the ledge, and I started to hook us in.

Something was bugging me. I looked at the knot between the two pitons. The problem with a knot such as the one I had tied is that, if one piton fails, you will fail. So I retied the knot more securely.

My buddies and I were clipped in, and we all wanted to get going as it was getting darker and darker. The way I had tied the knot did seem "good enough." But something in the back of my head told me to stop. So I did.

We all unclipped and I retied that knot once again. Then we clipped ourselves in again and started the climb down.

The moment I put my weight onto the line, the first piton popped out and hit me smack in the middle of my helmet. Had I not unclipped and retied that knot, I would have died on that ledge. My life rushed through my mind, and I suddenly and irrevocably understood the danger of "GOOD ENOUGH."

When I tied the knot that first time, I had decided that it was NOT good enough and I retied the knot once again.

I still have that piton that had popped out. I brought it with me today because I thought you might like to see it. As for the other piton, the one that had saved my life,....well, it's still in a crack on the ledge in Laurel Cliffs, doing its job.

I came back to work, and everything had new meaning for me. Retying my knots became a sort of metaphor. I realised that in every job I did, every project I touched, I was making piton decisions every time. I was deciding with every one of those moves, whether "good enough" was good enough for me.

I picked that story for today because I think we are facing a similar climb as a company. And we are making "piton" decisions every day.

| The Essential Nature of Body Language |

Most people are not consciously aware of how they move their hands or how they stand when speaking with or in front of others. It is important to recognise that your physical movements produce an internal response in you, the presenter, and your audience. For example, if you tend to keep your hands in front of you or grab the lectern for dear life, the audience may see how fearful or uncomfortable you are. That can negatively affect how they receive your ideas and proposals. On the other hand, if you appear comfortable and open, it may help your audience feel more warmly towards you and what you are saying.

And, while talking with your hands extensively will convey your enthusiasm for the subject, it can also be distracting for your audience.

Body language is such a vital form of communication that it can make or break your presentation. It is so powerful that it can reinforce your verbal message or contradict it.

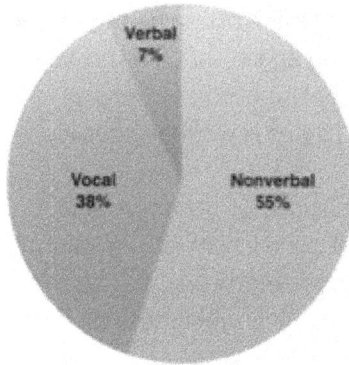

In fact, Mehrabian's rule suggests that communication relies less on the words you use and the tone of your voice than it does on your body language.

As an essential part of emotional intelligence, body language is extremely helpful in bonding with your audience, whether large or small. Deliberate body language shows that you are in control and happy to be where you are, doing what you are doing. Also, changing your body position can affect the chemicals in your body and make you feel more confident. Using the right body language can also increase your internal energy and better resonate with your audience.

On the other hand, the wrong body language can cause dire results. A good presentation can easily crumble when a presenter says one thing with their lips and sends an entirely different message with their body. As you saw in the first chapter, bad body language played a huge part in Richard Nixon losing a critical US presidential debate.

He appeared nervous and uncertain on television, while his opponent, John F. Kennedy, appeared calm and confident. In fact, Nixon's body language blunders cost him the election within the first 20 seconds of the debate. As mentioned in the first chapter, he instantly triggered distrust with the audience because he did not even make eye contact. Instead, he turned his head to look towards Kennedy, which automatically signaled submission and positioned Kennedy as the alpha candidate. Nixon tightly gripped the arm of his chair revealing nervousness and his clenched fist displayed aggression. The nonverbal cues in this debate were so powerful that Nixon himself went on to admit, "I should have remembered that a picture is worth a thousand words."

While it may feel unnatural or uncomfortable to use your hands and stance to project self-confidence and positivity at first, by the time you are unconsciously competent you will be able to naturally use nonverbal communication to strengthen your message.

| Eight Types of Body Language |

Scientific research and theory into nonverbal communication first became popular when it was introduced to the public by Charles Darwin with the 1872 publication, The Expression of the Emotions in Man and Animals. Since then, the way we speak without speaking has been analysed extensively, and research reveals there are eight types of nonverbal communication. These eight types are facial expression, gestures, tone, posture, proxemics (personal space), eye contact, haptics (body contact), and appearance. When you practise your presentation, you will want to take notice of each type. You may find it helpful to tape yourself or ask a colleague to watch you practise so that you can better identify where you need to make adjustments.

| Know Your Current Body Language |

Make a conscious effort to notice what types of movement come naturally to you. You can do this most easily in situations where you are relaxed and unselfconscious, such as chatting with friends or family.

Specifically, become aware of how your body reacts when you get animated, especially when telling stories and jokes or discussing a topic you are passionate about. Take note of how you hold yourself, move, and gesture. Whatever you are doing is the way you use body language when you are relaxed and appropriately activated. While you will want to adapt some "power" moves and poses that are described later in this chapter, you will be wise to stay away from gestures that seem forced or unnatural.

| Key Body Language Tips |

Too many speakers move, or do not move, in ways that work against their own effectiveness. You have seen them time and time again: the still-as-a-statue speaker behind the lectern, the wanderer, or the tiger-in-the-cage pacer, among others.

At The Genard Method of performance-based public speaking training in Boston, body language is a key element of all of their executive speech coaching and team presentation training. Below are four key areas that they also include in their work with clients. Being familiar with them in terms of your own presentation style will help you practise powerful body language techniques.

1. Making movement and gestures work.

The reason any of us use gestures in a presentation is to amplify or support what we are saying through physical expression of that idea. Think of the times you have been excited about something you were talking about—did you not incorporate some movement to show that passion?

Indeed, it may well have been difficult to express what you were saying without any movement.

However, if your gestures are too frequent, too similar, or weak to the point of vagueness, make them cleaner, more defined, and fewer in number. Your message will resonate much more strongly with listeners if, when you say something really important, you make an emphatic gesture no one has seen up to that point.

There is an easy gesture-related mnemonic to help you keep your audience engaged and attentive. It is NODS, which stands for Neutral, Open, Defined, and Strong. Genard suggests beginning in a neutral position with hands at your sides (it may feel awkward at first; however, it looks fine). That keeps you open to your audience, allowing influence to flow freely in both directions. You will probably want to use that gesture sparingly, along with defined or "clean" hand movements that are strong. Follow the NODS formula and your upper body movement will always support and amplify what you say.

2. Using space wisely.

When you speak in public, a certain amount of space on the stage or at the front of the room is yours by right. You will want to command that space and show your audience that you are comfortable being in the leadership position. And, while you will not want to "roam" unnecessarily, you will want to move easily over a reasonable amount of space at the front of the room.

Speakers who stand like a statue in one place or those who wander aimlessly are ignoring the value of purposeful movement in public speaking. Distance by itself can create an understanding in another person (or audience) concerning how you feel about them. Speech experts often recognise three measures of the distance between speaker and listener(s): intimate, conversational, and public. Which of these levels of distance you maintain between you and those you speak to depends on the situation and your relationship with them.

One of the keys to moving well as a speaker is to employ *purposeful movement.* There has to be a reason why you are walking from Point A to Point B. Approaching the PowerPoint screen to point something is out is one example of purposeful movement; another is taking a step or two towards a questioner in the audience or moving to physically connect with people on one side of the room. So is one of the acting techniques known as coming "down-centre" (as actors label the space in the centre of the stage closest to the audience), which is the most powerful spot to deliver a strong opening and closing.

There is an easy way to link movement and message: occupy a different part of your performance space for each main point you are discussing. Let us say you will be talking about three main points in your presentation. Start down-centre for your introduction. Then move to Position One for your first point. Gesture naturally when you get there without diluting the strength of that thought by moving *during* it. Move to Position Two for your next point, and then make a similar move for your last idea. You will want to come back down-centre for a strong conclusion. Your audience will find it much easier to retain your main points if you move this way than if you wander, pace, or even stand stock-still while you make each of them.

Too much movement, however, can be distracting, and can feel unfocused. You will want to move only when you cannot NOT *move any longer.* That is, if you create the conditions for the movement or gesture, it will emerge naturally, and at just the right moment.

There is that word again: natural. Body language is a powerful tool of public speaking. But it can only be effective if it does not look staged, stiff, or planned. You are, without a doubt, one of the most important visual aids you possess as a speaker. Make your physical expression emerge from your own need to communicate, just as you make it part of your message, and you will truly be someone worth watching as much as you are a speaker worth listening to.

Is your performance space small? That is not a problem; simply take a step or two each time, rather than striding across the stage as if you were last speaking in a large lecture hall.

I am not saying *plan* how you move; simply that you will want to be aware of when and how you are moving while practising your presentation. You may even want to make notes for yourself about actions that felt right and comfortable, as well as which statements you want to emphasise through movement.

3. Dealing with objects and technology.

Good actors use props, while bad actors are used by their props. Inexperienced presenters can become discombobulated. When you deal with objects in a presentation, from a remote clicker to a handout to the slide screen itself, find a way to help that object further your message and its impact. Practising with your props beforehand will help you feel more comfortable. Also, checking the equipment before your presentation will assure that everything is in working order.

4. Having an expressive face.

We human beings rely on facial expressions to make judgments concerning the trustworthiness, motives, and emotions of others. Audience members depend upon your facial expressions to augment meaning. If you do not have an expressive face, work with a mirror to create a link between what you are trying to express verbally, and how your facial expressions make your meaning clear. As part of your practice, give your entire talk without a sound coming out of your mouth even though you form all the words, letting your face do all the communicating.

| Six Common Body Language Mistakes |

When you are in front of an audience, a lack of confidence can compel you to nervously rush through your material or use your body in a way that is not beneficial to your message. Practising proper body language will make you more relaxed and in control. You will want to especially look to correct the following commonly made body language mistakes.

1. Rubbing hands: Clasping your hands, rubbing them together or fidgeting with them indicates nervousness. These movements may give your audience the impression that you are uncomfortable and do not believe what you are saying. Experts suggest keeping your arms to your side in an open manner. Use your hands to deliver calculated, concise gestures in conveying your words.

2. Crossing your arms: This gives others the sense that you are unimpressed or something is amiss. It is a defensive position that can easily put distance between you and your audience. Be conscious of keeping your arms open and away from your body, as this open gesture is inviting, trusting, and gives the audience a sense of peace and confidence.

3. Avoiding eye contact: When you focus your eyes, it [14] "helps you concentrate. When your eyes wander, they take in random, extraneous images that are sent to your brain, and slow it down. When you fail to make eye contact with your listeners, you look less authoritative, less believable, and less confident. When you do not look people in the eye, they are less likely to look at you. And when they stop looking at you, they start thinking about something other than what you are saying, and when that happens, they stop listening. When you look them in the eye, they are more likely to look at you, more likely to listen to you, and more likely to buy you and your message."

[14] 10 Reasons Eye Contact Is Everything in Public Speaking.., http://www.inc.com/sims-wyeth/10-reasons-why-eye-contact-can-change-peoples-perc.

Briefly establish eye contact to a comfortable degree with everyone, when you make a point. Keep it short and sincere without being too quick. You can start with the people who initially catch your eye, and people who seem to be enjoying the presentation, since that will make you less nervous. However as soon as possible, try to look at the ones with whom you are less comfortable making eye contact. Remember, it is not about you; it is about your audience members. Eye contact makes them feel good, and that will start to show on their faces.

4. Poor posture: Among the many attributes of body language, posture is one that speaks the loudest. A slouched back, drooped shoulders or a head continuously tilted to one side indicate surrender, not a willingness to take on the world in a worthy endeavor.. Keep your head high and legs strong. These postures will not only make you look confident on the outside; they will also make you feel more confident on the inside.

5. Annoying movements: Pacing back and forth and moving your arms and legs quickly are common distractions that will not fare well when you try to inspire and persuade your audience in a presentation. Navigate the room with slow confidence. Send a more positive message by slowly moving across the front of the entire crowd, and standing in one place as much as possible.

6. Forgetting to smile: People will judge you and the content of your speech more favourably if you use an open, friendly, encouraging tone (as opposed to an aggressive, sarcastic or bored one). A good way to make your tone more friendly and warm is to smile while you speak. Even a slight upturn of the corners of your mouth can make the sound of your voice more appealing — even over the phone. Of course, smiling is not always appropriate, especially if you are discussing a serious issue. Remember that inserting emotion into your voice (whatever emotion it may be) can do wonders.

| Power Poses |

Some exciting new research has emerged regarding using body language to strengthen your power as a speaker. It has to do with social psychologist Amy Cuddy's research into "power poses." Cuddy discussed her findings in a talk, "Your Body Language Shapes Who You Are."

According to Cuddy's research, assuming a powerful pose before participating in a high-stress situation demanding peak performance increases one's level of testosterone (the dominance hormone), and decreases cortisol (a stress hormone). In other words, assuming a power pose makes one feel more able to control the situation and experience less stress. Therefore, consider beginning with a power pose. Then use movement throughout the rest of your presentation. This will show that you are a powerful presenter that stands out from the crowd- literally.

| Talk With Your Hands |

Controlled use of power hand gestures can make a strong point stronger and drive a message home. They work best when they come naturally.

IMPORTANCE: To place positive emphasis on something, consider using a hand chop as you say the word.

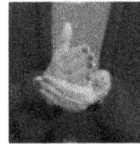

ALL-ENCOMPASSING: Moving your hand from side to side explains the entirety of a concept. For example, you may make this gesture when saying "We take care of all of our clients."

REALLY LISTEN NOW: When you want your audience's full attention and concentration, you may choose to use the stop gesture in which you hold your hand out, palm up and facing the audience.

This gesture is most often made when being literal, as in "Now let's stop and think about that for a moment." It cues them to stop and pay attention.

MINIMAL: When you want to show something as really minor, you can hold your hand up and place the thumb and second figure relatively close together. You can say, "Not having a patent is a minor issue for us."

WE ARE ON THE SAME PAGE: When you want comradery with the audience, you can place your hands somewhat close together and move them to and fro. This helps remind the audience that you are on their side. You may say something like, "Bringing consistency to your business is a plan we have to work on together."

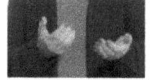

WHAT DO YOU THINK: Whenever you ask for feedback from the audience or want them to raise their hands, be sure to non-verbally open your body. This is how you ask for feedback: "So, tell me, have any of you had this experience before?" The palms-out gesture shows that you are receptive to their thoughts.

COMPLETE: There are two ways you can say you are done with something or doing away with something. The first is the finished gesture as indicated on the right. Or, you can take a concept and literally throw it away – by moving your hand from a high position across your body to the right in a downward diagonal line. "Most companies charge their clients for this – we don't believe in that."

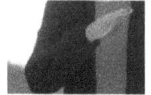

UNITY: When bringing things together, you can mesh your hands. "We bring all the elements of your home together to make it look beautiful." This is also a great way to communicate working together. You can say, "The marketing and sales team will be working together on this."

EMPATHY: When you tell an intimate or a personal story, keep your hands close to your chest or touch your heart. For example, "My passion for interior design is why I started my business."

NEW FUTURE: When you talk about the *New Future,* and you are promising the audience something, always gesture towards them. This wakes them up and makes them hopeful for their future. For example, "Our marketing services will create consistency in your business."

EXPERT: Research has shown that putting your fingertips together like this makes for a very powerful pose that positions you as an expert. It makes you feel confident and builds credibility with the audience right away. They feel confident in you and allow you to take the lead.

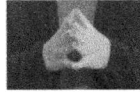

When you intentionally use this gesture in situations where you are feeling tense or nervous, it does two things. First, when you intentionally make the gesture, you start to feel more confident and in charge. As importantly, the person who sees you do it gets the feeling you seem to know what you are talking about.

Use these body language gestures only to emphasise very important points. The less frequently you use them during the presentation, the more effective they will be. When you have your hands constantly moving, you will lose the audience.

CHAPTER 7
PREPARATION
PART TWO

| **Chapter 7 -** Preparation Part Two |

The human voice is an instrument we all play. It is arguably the most powerful sound in the world. It can start a war or say "I love you." It can make you smile, or it can make you cry. It can bore you to death, or it can inspire you! And yet, many people have the experience that, when they speak, people do not listen to them. Why is that? It may be because those speakers have not yet learned how to tune their instrument.

We have all sat through a presentation or speech and realised that we were not absorbing any of the information because of the speaker's voice. Perhaps they were talking too fast. Perhaps they ran their words together, spoke in a boring monotone that made us sleepy, or spoke in such a low volume that we were not able to hear clearly. Conversely, we have all heard at least one person in our lives whose voice is so beautiful and rich that we enjoy listening to them speak, sometimes regardless of what they are actually saying.

What is the one overall vocal technique that differentiates powerful speakers from merely good ones and ineffective ones? It is variety. According to an analysis of media appearances by 120 top financial communicators, the sound of a speaker's voice matters twice as much as the content of the message. Speaking in a monotone makes your proposals sound boring and unimportant. Learning to modulate your sound level, pace, tone, and timbre, on the other hand, will keep your audience interested and attentive, as well as give import to your critical recommendations and the facts that support them.

Note: Aim for projection, not getting louder and higher. This involves intention and focus — being aware of where you want to direct your voice rather than merely volume alone.

While learning how to modulate your voice and developing perfect vocal intonation and diction can be a lifelong task, a beautiful sounding voice can be obtained in a relatively short amount of time.

All you need is a little guidance and some dedicated practice.

Here are the key areas to focus on when learning to modulate your voice and speaking style.

| Speak Up |

The content of a presentation can be riveting; however, if it cannot be heard or absorbed it is all for naught. Do not be shy and soft spoken when giving a presentation. If you tend to whisper, mumble or speak with your head down, it is likely that your audience will not hear a thing. When you speak too quietly, it is also much easier for people to talk over you or ignore you. However, this does not mean you need to shout. The point is to be heard, but not perceived as angry or argumentative.

According to a research study performed by San Diego State and Columbia Business School, listeners naturally associate voices that vary in volume, with a tendency towards louder volumes, with authority. (Positioning and presenting yourself as an expert increases the likelihood that your audience will comply with your requests.) Hence, the next time you present, convey your expertise by speaking up, so people can hear you clearly. However, be careful. Do not be so loud that you drive your audience out of the room.

Conversely, there are times when speaking softly is warranted by the situation. Susan Cain employed a subtle style while giving one of the most illustrious talks at TED 2012. During her talk, "The Power of Introverts," she spoke with a gentle yet persuasive voice. Her approach was in perfect harmony with her topic and the audience. She delivered her core message in a way that resonated with fellow introverts when she wished them "the courage to speak softly."

Note: An analysis of the most famous TED talks revealed that successful TED speakers have 30.5% higher vocal variety than less popular TED speakers. Therefore, to increase your charisma and credibility, increase the amount of fluctuation in your voice tone, volume, and pitch.

| Set the Pace |

Many speakers talk too quickly, making it difficult for the members of the audience to register and process the information being presented. You may find yourself speaking more quickly than is usual for you because you are nervous or because you are worried that you will not have sufficient time to get all the information covered within your allotted time. Slowing down allows you to suitably explain concepts and gather your thoughts before moving on.

However, speaking too slowly is also a detriment to delivering a power presentation as you may appear to have no energy or passion for your subject. Varying your speed makes your speech more interesting and your meaning clear beyond all doubt. As an example, a speaker may say something very, very quickly to heighten the sense of excitement, and then slow right down to place emphasis on a critical point of information or a conclusion. Pausing works the same way, and a pause... can be immensely powerful. Needless to say, it is not necessary to fill every moment or transition with content, ums and ahs.

| Tone and Timbre |

A research study from Duke University School of Business shows the earning power of a voice extends to male CEOs. The research looked at 792 male CEOs and found that CEOs with deeper voices manage larger companies, make more money and tend to be retained longer. (It is not unreasonable to assume that a study among women will have similar results about tone and authority.) Stay in the lowest register of your natural voice for most of your presentation. Use a higher pitch in small doses, if at all, and only for effect.

Timbre is the way your voice feels. Again, research shows that society prefers voices that are rich, smooth, and warm, like hot chocolate.

If you do not have that kind of voice, it is not the end of the world, because you can train! When you hire an expert coach, there are amazing things you can do with breathing, with posture, and with exercises to improve the timbre of your voice.

| Resonance |

Your voice originates in your vocal cords and then resonates through your chest, throat, and head as it comes out of your mouth. To enhance vocal tone, you have to "open up" the throat, and head cavities to allow the voice to resonate. You may want to try right now to hold your nose and say "Many mighty men making much money in the moonshine" with as much force as possible. Then immediately let go of your nose and say the same phrase. You will immediately hear the difference in the force of your vocal sound. Practising humming is an excellent way of improving resonance.

| Pitch |

Pitch is an integral part of the human voice. The pitch of a voice is defined as the "rate of vibration of the vocal folds." The sound of the voice changes as the rate of vibrations varies. As the number of vibrations per second increases, so does the pitch, meaning the voice will sound higher.

Even a powerful presenter with a compelling message can be hurt by an unattractive pitch. Margaret Thatcher, for example, initially spoke with a high-pitched voice and had to be trained by a voice expert to lower her pitch.

To find your optimum pitch, place your hand on your chest, at heart level. Breathe with your diaphragm and say a long "Oooooooh" starting with a high pitch and swooping down to the lowest pitch you have and then up again.

Pay attention to the vibration in your chest; there will be a specific pitch level at which you will feel more vibration than another. This is your optimum level of pitch. The more vibration you can achieve the better.

Note: Pitch often goes along with pace to indicate enthusiasm and excitement; however, you can get a similar result by varying your pitch. For example, asking "Where did you leave my keys?" in your normal pitch is non-confrontational and direct. Asking the same question in a higher pitch may indicate anger or even fear.

| Prosody |

This is a term you may not have heard of before. It is the sing-song within our conversation, that is the consistent jingle in rhythm and pattern of pitch which we use in order to impart meaning. People who speak all on one note (monotone) are really rather hard to listen to because they have no prosody at all. On the other hand, too much sing-song does not come across well either. Therefore, use prosody judiciously. Repetitive prosody, when every sentence ends as if it were a question even if it is a statement, restricts your ability to communicate.

| Be Consistent |

A presentation is at its most powerful when the speaker integrates body language, facial expressions, and tone of voice. People have an innate ability to pick up on nonverbal cues and, when there is a disconnect between the speaker's voice and facial expressions, it can confuse the audience and create skepticism. You can probably recall this phenomenon from a political debate you may have watched in the past!

Specifically, when your facial expressions communicate one emotion, while the tone of your voice conveys an opposite message, your audience will become skeptical as a result of this Neural Dissonance.

Inconsistency between your facial expressions and your voice projection can damage your credibility and decrease your effectiveness as a persuasive speaker. Communicate credibility by aligning your voice and your facial expressions with the emotion you are trying to convey with your words.

| Do Not Forget to Breathe |

The majority of people breathe too quickly and shallowly when they speak, which results in a more high-pitched, nasal tone. If you are one of the many, you may choose to begin breathing exercises — especially deep breathing exercises — well before your presentation. Remember that your breath needs to come from your diaphragm, not from your chest.

When speaking, try to breathe at the end of every sentence with the intent of taking in enough air to get through the next sentence without having to pause for breath. This will also give your listeners a chance to absorb what you are saying.

Note: Sitting or standing up straight, with your chin up and your shoulders back, will help you to breathe deeper and project your voice more easily. It will also give you an air of confidence as you speak.

| The Croaking Voice (The Fry) |

This is another term related to the voice that may be unfamiliar to you, although the sound most certainly is: the creaking, drawn out tone that emerges when speaking below your normal projection. According to some studies, the vocal fry hurts first impressions of both men and women. Other studies, however, have concluded that vocal fry is often viewed as authoritative by people under 40 years of age, while people 40 years of age and older interpret the vocal fry as a negative speaking trait.

Therefore, it is important to know when to fry and when not fry, based on your audience.

Additionally, people tend to talk from the back of their heads rather than from the resonators which are behind the cheek bones. Many young people speak in their throat, and that can be difficult to listen to as well. It can also be uncomfortable; if you pretend to drink a glass of water, saying glug, glug, glug you will find that the sound hurts your throat. To correct this issue, open your mouth very wide and use both your teeth and mouth when speaking. You may find a yawning exercise helpful when practising, and during your pre-presentation warm up.

With so many studies telling you how to speak, knowing the best way to communicate can be confusing. If you are overwhelmed by the variety of suggestions for speakers, remember that authenticity always wins. First and foremost, you need to always be true to yourself.

| Tuning Up Your Voice |

To understand how your voice makeover will influence your audience's perception of you as a speaker, rehearse your speech in front of a small group of people who will give you candid feedback on the impact of your voice. Feedback from people within your target audience will provide you with the clearest path towards enhancing your voice for public speaking success. You may also choose to record your voice using your mobile or computer. This can be very constructive as it may help with enunciation as well as tone. Keep in mind that many people are taken aback when initially hearing their own voice on a recording as it is likely to sound quite different than it does in your head.

| Consider Seeing a Voice Coach |

If you want to improve your speaking voice, consult a coach. They can identify your individual speech issues and help you to correct them. A voice coach is also a good idea if you have a colloquial accent that you would like to minimise or eliminate.

| Practice Makes Perfect |

In the US, a pottery class teacher divided her students into two groups. The first half of the class were told that "At the end of this terms, your grade will be given on the weight of pots that you create. Here is a weighing scale and, at the end of the class, whoever's total of production of pots weighs the most will get the highest grade." The other half of the class was told that they would be evaluated on their most finished piece of pottery.

The group that was told "sheer weight" was the primary criteria for grading produced five, six, seven pots a day. They tried random experiments and weird things. Their hands were on clay from the first moment on. On the other hand, the half of the class who were told they would be evaluated on the most finished pot, read, thought, and talked about the concepts. They talked more, read more and were very philosophical. They also went to galleries to look at other people's pots. These students didn't even touch clay until about three days before the end of the class.

The result of this teacher's experiment? All of the best pots were made by the group that focused on weight.

I always suggest to my clients that they rehearse over and over, meaning you can never practise too much. Whenever possible, rehearse in the room in which you will be presenting, using the screen, computer and other electronic devices and tools that you will be using during the real presentation.

Ask people to sit in on your rehearsals and provide constructive criticism on everything from the size of the type on your slides to your use of hand symbols and power poses.

| Lose the Filler |

Rehearsing your presentation many times will help you decide which body language and hand gestures feel most authentic and natural. It will also allow you to identify and eliminate the verbal ticks most speakers use when a pause will serve better. Words and phrases, including um, er, you know, like and anyway, are distracting and their use makes you seem uncomfortable and less competent.

It is likely that you will be surprised at how much these ticks appear in normal speech, all because people are afraid of the silence that comes between phrases and sentences. I had a client whose rehearsals were recorded, and she was horrified to hear how many times she used filler words throughout her speech. We then worked really hard until it became comfortable for her to speak using pauses instead of interjecting "um" and "you know" throughout her talk. She quickly learned, there is great power in the silence that results from a pause. It gives the audience a chance to reflect and can give dramatic emphasis to something you have said.

At its best, the well-timed pause can be as effective, if not more so, than any "magic" word you may choose to use. Mark Twain said, *"The right word may be effective, but no word was ever as effective as a rightly timed pause."*

Many people do not realise that they have a verbal tick until they see or hear themselves. That is another reason it is important to record yourself or have others listen as you rehearse. Becoming self-aware and really hearing how bad tick sounds will help you to remove them and sound more fluent.

| Rehearse and Rehearse for Success |

The Beatles were known to have honed their skills as a band by playing almost nightly in Hamburg, Germany during the early 1960s. In Outliers, journalist, author and speaker Malcolm Gladwell posits and then proves through examples (such as The Beatles) that it takes at least 10,000 hours to become truly expert at something. It is by doing something over and over again that we become both proficient and comfortable doing it.

Before we do just about anything, we need to learn how to do it. There are four steps in the learning process; we start out being 1) unconsciously incompetent, which means that we do not know how much we do not know about something, and then move through the stages of 2) consciously knowing we are incompetent and need to get better at it to 3) being consciously competent, meaning we are good at the action yet need to think about what we are doing as we are doing it. 4) Rehearsal is the fourth step in the learning process, the one in which we go from consciously competent to unconsciously competent, meaning that we do it naturally, without thinking about it. It is very much like riding a bicycle or driving a car in that, with sufficient practice, it becomes natural, and muscle memory takes over, so you do not need to think about the steps involved.

An actor's creative process works in the same way. They begin reading through the material "cold" together with the other members of the cast; next, comes preliminary stage movement while still working with the script in hand; this is called "on book." Once they have studied and learned their lines, the actors move "off book" which allows for more creativity. However, the performance may still lack depth because the actor needs to remember the words as well as say them. After sufficient rehearsal, the actor becomes more able to be in the character as the lines become second nature. They may then add nuance to the character's actions, improvise or otherwise make their performance more natural and authentic.

Sitting hunched over a computer, reading, and mumbling is not rehearsing, and it will do little towards making you the master of your presentation. It is a good idea to create a space in your home that represents the "stage" perhaps with a small row of chairs in front of you or a TV screen behind. If practising at work, book the conference room rather than talking quietly to yourself at your desk.

Ask a few friends around to be the audience, or put some cushions around and pretend they are your audience. Do the presentation for real with the gestures and passion at full-force, going through every word that you will say. Do not under rehearse. You want to be on the stage as though you have done the speech before. Muscle memory is with you. Voice memory is with you, and everything is working for you.

Let's assume that you are happy with your slides and any other materials you intend to use for demonstration. You are now ready to map out the final details for your speech. For example, are you planning to project your slides onto a screen at one end of the room, have your small audience sit in front of a computer or review and take notes of a handout? Each has its advantages although, typically, a projected image works best for a big group.

Next, knowing that you do not want to have to turn away from your audience to read a screen, decide if you will be most comfortable glancing at your own computer, a tablet or even old-school note cards. (Cards are preferred over a piece of paper because if you are slightly nervous and your hand is shaking paper vibrates, and the associated sound really amplifies so that everybody in the audience can see that your hand is shaking. Cards, however, are quite stable and you can hold them with both hands.)

Whichever device you choose, do not write out your entire speech; stick to your bullet points. Otherwise, you will find yourself, head leaning downward, reading every word and worried about missing a phrase or losing your place. It is far better to maintain eye contact with your audience while appearing self-confident and in charge of delivering your message.

| Know Everything is in Place |

The other part of preparation is making sure that everything you need will be available. That means everything. Introduce yourself in advance to the people who will be preparing the room and tell them what you will need. You cannot over-specify. For example, if you need 14.9 projection, then you need to tell them that, or if you are coming with HD projection, you need to tell them that as well. Make sure the IT and equipment team know if you have video, embedded sound, or need a microphone (and, if you do, whether you prefer a handheld one or a headset). They will also need to know if you are bringing your own computer and if you need any special materials to hook your computer into their system. All of these things need to be specified.

CHAPTER 8
PRESENTATION

| **Chapter 8 -** Presentation |

Your presentation actually starts before you walk on the stage and start talking. Make sure that you arrive early and check everything — especially the technology and the stage or room. If you are giving out materials, make sure they are in place and that everything you need on stage is there for your demonstration (if you have one). Expect the worst and have backup plans. In addition, conduct your check before any audience members have entered the room, even if that means being at the venue or client at seven in the morning or even the night before.

| **Do a Run-Through** |

Last year, I spoke at a four-speaker meeting where one speaker was immediately followed by the next. The speaker before me was not using a projector, so I had no chance to check the technology beforehand. I was unable to confirm that the machines were working properly, if my slides were in place or if the sound system was working. It was a disaster, and I actually had to send for a technician while I was speaking. Likewise, be prepared to speak without any audio-visual aids in the unthinkable situation of a power cut.

Whenever possible, conduct a tech run-through with the crew in attendance to make sure any potential problems are dealt with well ahead of your speaking time. Remember to introduce yourself to the tech team and try to remember their names. If you are presenting in a conference room or executive office, check where each client usually likes to sit so as to assure that the most important people can read the screen clearly. If you are speaking in a larger venue, check the stage, the walk on space and the path you are to use to exit the stage. Be clear with your stage directions; check the whole room and make sure it looks appropriate.

Again, expect the worst and have contingency plans. *When I was teaching drama to children, we once had a performance in which they had to go on without any scenery; there wasn't even a backdrop. I had to improvise. I said to the parents "We are going to transport you to a tropical island. Imagine a palm tree over here..."*

Bring your presentation on a backup USB stick just in case something goes wrong with the equipment. Likewise, if there is a power cut, be prepared to speak without any audio-visual aids. If this happens, being able to stand and deliver your presentation without audio-visual aids is a very powerful thing.

| Warm Up |

We all know a car needs to be warmed up and the engine needs to be revved to get maximum performance. It is equally important to warm up our voices and to get ourselves into the moment. Otherwise, you are not fully oiled and ready to go when you walk on stage.

Warming up your voice is very important. It can prevent starting off with a croak, crack or something similar. You may want to use the same exercises you practised with at home, or you may choose to try the one that I like to do before I go on stage. There are eight of them, and you can view them on my website.

There are some other things you can do to warm up and get yourself energised to be a powerful presenter. The power poses referenced in Chapter 6 can actually release testosterone in your system, making you feel bigger than you are because they are open and expansive; think of the arms-stretched-out-wide winner's pose often used by athletes.

According to Amy Cuddy, the point is that going to a quiet place such as the washroom and doing a power pose will give you the hormones you need to feel strong and confident immediately. This is also a good way to reduce nerves and pre-speaking jitters.

| Handling "Stage Fright" |

Remember this joke from Seinfeld: *If you go to a funeral, you would be better off in the casket than doing the eulogy?* What if it is not a joke? When researchers interviewed study participants on their top fears, speaking in public was actually ranked before death. It is a common problem, so much so that the American Institute of Mental Health says around 72% of people suffer from glossophobia, the fear of public speaking.

There are several reasons many of us find public speaking scary. We fear embarrassment. We fear that we are going to mess up. We fear that we are going to say something silly. We fear that we are going to freeze and forget what to say. We fear we are going to be judged and ridiculed. And maybe the worst one of all is that you may feel you are going to be rejected, which is the fear that people are not going to like your ideas, and they are not going to accept who you are.

The good news is that these fears are merely in your head. There is always a way to overcome your greatest fears *(yes, even public speaking)!* The key lies in setting those fears aside and taking action anyway. The brain can only hold one thought at a time so you can distract it from the fear more easily than you may imagine. Let me share a story about what can happen when you experience the fear, yet take action anyway:

When Richard Paul Evans wrote his first book The Christmas Box, *it was simply a gift of love to his two young daughters. Later, he made photocopies for family and friends, and word spread quickly about this heartwarming tale. Spurred on by this positive reaction, Rick sought a publisher for the book. When there were no takers, Rick decided to publish it himself. To promote the book, he took a booth at a regional American Booksellers Association conference where, among other activities, celebrity authors were signing books at one end of the exhibit hall.*

Rick noticed these celebrity authors were the only ones getting attention from the press. He also noticed when the next group of celebrities arrived for their scheduled time, one author had failed to arrive. With his fear being crowded out by his courage and commitment to his dream, Rick decided to take a leap. He picked up two boxes of books, walked towards the empty chair, sat down and began to sign.

Seeing him at the table, a woman from the show approached him to ask him to leave. Undaunted, Evans looked up, and before she could speak said, "Sorry I'm late." The stunned woman just looked at him and asked, "Can I get you something to drink?"

The next year Evans was the premier author at the show as his book had climbed to #1 on the New York Times best-seller list. Since then The Christmas Box has sold more than eight million copies in 18 languages and has been made into an Emmy Award-winning CBS television movie. The book, which had previously been rejected by several major publishing houses, was eventually purchased by Simon and Schuster for a record $4.2 million.

Conversely, one cannot be too overconfident before taking the stage. Evans' bravado worked well given the circumstances, because he was able to rise to the occasion once he got into the celebrity section. Big egos think they can "get up there and wing it" or, worse, what the Americans call "phoning it in."

Here are a few of the most effective techniques that I practise with my clients before their big moments.

Visualisation

As per the hypnotherapist Marisa Peers, the brain does not actually know if an experience is real or imagined. Visualisation is based on using your imagination to form a mental image of yourself as a successful presenter. Seeing yourself take a sequence of steps, beginning with the moment you enter the room through to the moment you receive the applause, will help you let go of your fear.

If you have not worked with visualisation techniques before you may be skeptical. However, it really works! Research proves it. A study conducted at Harvard University divided participants into two groups, both of which were presented with a piece of unfamiliar piano music. One group received a keyboard and was told to practise. The second group was instructed to only read the music and imagine playing it. When their brain activity was assessed, both groups showed expansion in the motor cortex, even though the second group had never touched a keyboard.

Try it for yourself. Find a quiet spot where you will be undisturbed, sit down and focus on your breathing for a while as you relax. Next, imagine you are watching a film or a play of you making the forthcoming presentation exactly as you want it to be — word perfect and poised, with you in control and having the desired impact on your audience. The more vivid your images are, the more effective the technique will be and the quicker you will start to reduce your fear of public speaking.

Once you have watched yourself achieve success, step into the scene as though you are looking out onto the audience through your own eyes —remember, you have just completed a very successful presentation, so enjoy the feeling and really get in touch with it. Next, become the film director. Mentally step back out of the experience and make any changes to the film that will make it even better. Then wind the clock forward and keep the film running in your head so you can also see the benefits of making such a successful presentation.

It can take a little while to get used to this process of visualisation. Some people find it 'clicks' right away, while others find they may need a little more time and practise. Either way, it is a technique well worth implementing.

Relaxation Techniques

There are all sorts of ways to relax right before your presentation. For example, meditating beforehand is very effective. One of my favourite relaxation techniques, and one that I have seen work really well for my clients, is the T-Repeater. This is a technique developed by Steven Cohen, an award-winning speaker and instructor at Harvard. You start by turning your palms up and taking a deep breath in. Next, exhale making the t-sound (t-t-t-t-t-t). Doing this creates a sense of relaxation that will help you focus on your message right before you get in front of your audience.

Easing into Eye Contact

One of the reasons a lot of people are nervous when speaking is because other people are staring at them. It feels like everyone in the audience is judging the speaker, and the thought of looking those people in the eye can be intimidating. Rather than looking directly into their eyes, ease into eye contact. Try actually looking at a person's forehead or, if they are wearing glasses, at the rims of their glasses. Doing so creates the impression that you are looking at them, without actually looking at them. As you become more comfortable, of course, you can begin making actual eye contact with individuals in the audience.

| Taking the Stage |

Even if you are speaking on a serious subject, it is important to connect with your audience as soon as you take the stage, by smiling. Take a deep breath if you are nervous, to counteract the possibility of a quavery voice. Then, expand awareness by hooking onto people in the audience who appear to be enjoying your speech. You may want to assume a welcoming power pose in which you stand with your feet shoulder-width apart and your body stacked on top of everything else vertically. Relaxed shoulders will make you look and feel more confident. Also, you may choose to anchor yourself on stage for the beginning of your speech, and then use pacing and space judiciously, as walking around a lot can be very distracting.

| Stay Flexible |

Once upon a time, the Chamber of Commerce of a small rural town in Maine engaged a man from the agricultural college to give a talk to local farmers. The man was coming from a long way off, so he set out early on a sunny, but crisp, winter morning. Those were the days before satellites and weather predicting supercomputers. As the man traveled he began to encounter some unexpected elements, first in the form of fast-moving clouds, and then a light freezing rain turning to snow. However, the man had made a promise, and so he pressed on. Pretty soon the snow began to fall steadily, and that gave way to even more of the white stuff which was now being propelled by driving winds. A full blown north easterner had erupted, but the agricultural man had made a promise, so he plodded on.

Finally, just before the appointed time the man pushed himself with great effort through the door of the hall, stomped the snow off his shoes and hurried to the front of the room. The weather seemed to have delayed most of his audience, so he decided to wait. But after half an hour, only one lone soul had shuffled in. The man looked at his watch and then turned to the old man in overalls who appeared to be his only audience. "Well," said the man, "it's long past the time I am scheduled to begin, and the wind is howling outside; what do you think I should do?" The other fellow tugged on his overall and scratched his forehead with his thumbnail, then looked the agricultural man straight in the eye and said, "Sir, I may be just a poor farmer from down east, but there is one thing I do know. If only one horse comes to the barn, the man has still got to feed him." "O.K." replied the agricultural man, "I didn't mean any disrespect," and he stepped to the podium and commenced his talk.

As you may imagine, the agricultural man who was looking out at rows and rows of empty chairs began rather haltingly; however, it was his nature to press on, and he did. He had made a lot of speeches before and after a few minutes he came to ignore the peculiar circumstances and settled into his usual rhythm.

Pretty soon he felt completely comfortable, and he had just begun to hit his stride when he noticed that the farmer was looking at his watch. Suddenly, feeling self-conscious again, the agricultural man groped for a way to wind down his talk and awkwardly brought it to a conclusion. Then he walked over to the farmer and asked earnestly, "How do you think it went?" The farmer looked at his boots, put on his hat as if getting ready to go, and then met the agricultural man's eye. "Well, sir," he said, "I may be just a poor farmer from down east, but there is another thing that I do know. If only one horse comes to the barn the man doesn't give him the whole load."

This is a classic story related by Tony Jeary that illustrates the importance of learning how to be flexible and to tailor your presentation to fit your audience. The mistake made by the agriculture expert is one that inexperienced presenters make all too often. Like an actor who has not heard the director shout "cut" they plough ahead even when it has become clear that their audience is beginning to focus its attention elsewhere.

Masterful presenters, on the other hand, have the wherewithal to respond to their audience or to their own internal gyroscope, by adjusting their presentation style to keep their audience focused on their presentation. Some adjustments will be quite subtle and some profound. Keep in mind that making adjustments does not mean ad-libbing.

The underlying principle is the concept of planned spontaneity. The more prepared you are going into your presentation, the better positioned you will be to react spontaneously to your audience in a way that keeps getting your message across. The key is FLEXIBILITY.

| Involve Your Audience |

Presenters need to speak to the people in their audience, rather than at them. One of the most fundamental ways to do that is to include audience engagement. The topic, audience demographics, audience size, venue, and time will determine the way or the degree to which you engage with them.

Here are three effective ways to engage your listeners:

1. Engaging Activities

The most effective way to induce engagement from your audience, is to have them participate in an activity, rather than spending the entire talk simply listening to what you have to say. Your goal is to get people's blood flowing, mouths talking, and minds working. This will encourage your listeners to be alert and receptive to your message, especially as if they will feel as though they have a stake in your presentation.

The activities you choose can range from simple icebreakers to single-player or multiplayer games. Presenters need to give their audience members the chance to compete, work together, or simply have fun. It is not necessary for these activities to relate directly to your message; however, it will certainly help if they do. For example, Erik Wahl, a famous graffiti artist, asked audience members to demonstrate bravery by performing various activities that required them to step out of their comfort zone. As a reward, he gave away works of art that he painted during his presentation. Everyone wanted one, and Wahl knew that. He kept them engaged by creating suspense and excitement.

2. Live Demos

Master presenter Steve Jobs was, perhaps, the ultimate user of live demos. An example is when he first revealed FaceTime on the iPhone by calling his friend and colleague Jony Ive. Showing how a product works can break up the potential monotony of a long speech. It can be even more effective to get an audience member to do the demo.

That accomplishes multiple goals: it involves the audience in your presentation, it captures interest and builds suspense, and it demonstrates how other consumers will use your product or service. An audience member on stage can be the biggest advocate or the worst critic of your product when he or she sits down again.

A well thought out demo can also provide a "wow" moment that will keep the audience talking about your presentation long after it has ended. Intel CEO Brian Krzanich created a demonstration that impacted both his audience and at the level of media promotion by calling out the drones, literally. While demonstrating Intel's RealSense 3D camera, Krzanich invited members of a German company called Ascending Technologies to join him on stage as they controlled three drones. As the drones buzzed around him, Krzanich explained that the drones were able to avoid crashing into each other because they had depth-sensing cameras attached, powered, of course, by Intel.

Many presentations—especially product launches—lend themselves to such a wow moment. Executing a technological demo successfully can be a magical experience for an audience. However, it can risk your credibility if external factors such as spotty WiFi or malfunctioning equipment prevent it. This is why it is critical to rehearse, rehearse, and rehearse. Additionally, always have a backup plan.

3. Make Your Presentation Available Online

Hard copy information sheets or workbooks may help your presentation be interactive. However, these are, in today's world, old-fashioned and rather clumsy to deal with, particularly if you are speaking to a large group. Inspire audience interaction by posting your presentation on websites such as SlideShare and Prezi. This will allow your audience, as well as other users, to view the presentation, leave comments, or even follow along during the talk. Using technology to reach and engage your audience may seem distant or impersonal. However, it is a modern approach that has proven to be incredibly effective.

| Share the Stage |

Good presenters know that very few speakers can carry an entire hour without putting the audience to sleep. Therefore, smart leaders share the stage when appropriate. For example, Intel's Krzanich was joined by at least ten other speakers including Intel engineers, developers, and partners. Only 12 minutes into a keynote presentation, Ford's Mark Fields introduced Raj Nair, the company's chief technical officer. Nair was followed by a third speaker, a fourth speaker, and yet another speaker. You can keep a relatively long presentation moving by introducing more than one voice.

How does this work for a smaller group or shorter meeting? Advertising agencies, for example, often have the marketing person start off a presentation of new creative work by reviewing the selling strategy against which it was written. Then, the art director and writer may act out the commercial, sing the jingle or otherwise add some excitement to the presentation. Lastly, the marketing person or a research director may be called upon to recommend follow-up actions. Their call to action may be to conduct research among the product's target audience or to produce the commercial on location. Moving between speakers, back and forth, can work well in lots of situations, regardless of the size of a meeting.

| In Closing |

One crucial component that sometimes gets neglected is a strong call to action. Many speakers end with a call to action that is wishy-washy, hypothetical, or ill-constructed. Even worse, some speakers omit the call to action entirely.

A poor call to action undermines the effectiveness of your speech while a great one stirs your audience to act enthusiastically. It encourages them to do something because of what they heard you say, and it can range from something as literal as "Buy this product" to something as abstract as "Try using this idea at work."

Do not rush off when your speech is over. Thank everyone for listening. If you have been presenting to a small group of people, you may choose to shake hands and thank people individually. In a larger space, there is most likely to be applause; stay there and take a little recognition. Presenters who say thank you very much and rush off while the audience is still clapping are being quite rude.

| Lower Barriers to Action |

Most often, your call to action will be related to moving a work project ahead, selling a product or an idea, or asking the audience to take action. To help them act quickly, eliminate as many trivial and non-trivial barriers as you can. For example:

- *Do they need to sign up?*

- *Bring forms and pens and pass them out.*

- *Do they need to read additional information?*
  Bring handouts, copies of books, or website references.

- *Do they need approval before they can act?*
  As a first call to action, ask to organise a meeting with stakeholders.

- *Do they need to pay?*
  Accept as many forms of payment as possible.

A common psychological barrier is the perception that the suggested action is too big or too risky. This is a legitimate concern and is often best handled by dividing the call to action into several smaller and less risky actions. For example, "Train for a marathon." This may be a difficult call to action for a non-runner. A better call to action is to join a running club or train for a shorter race.

CHAPTER 9
DEBUNKING THE FIVE BIGGEST MYTHS ABOUT PRESENTING

CHAPTER 9

| **Chapter 9** - Debunking the Five Biggest Myths About Presenting |

Now that you have learned about many things you can do to improve your public speaking skills and become a powerful presenter, it is time to dispel the five common myths that seem to do more harm than good.

1. You can begin with a joke.

Humour is a great thing when done correctly, yet most executives, professionals and entrepreneurs lack both the skill and the practice to put a good joke across. Add to that the likely case of initial nerves that afflict most speakers, and you have a guaranteed failure. The executive delivers the joke feeling tense, the audience responds to the tension and not to the joke, and that makes the executive even more apprehensive. The audience begins to smell disaster and reacts accordingly. It is a vicious communications cycle, and it is quite hard to stop. Do not go for the joke; tell a story instead.

2. Too much rehearsal is bad for me.

People often try to avoid rehearsing, convincing themselves there are too many other tasks at hand. They use the excuse of 'not wanting to go stale' rather than making the time to rehearse. When it comes time to speak, they look unprepared, as if they are learning as they go. This makes them seem as anything other than authoritative. Their body unconsciously reveals their unease, and the audience interprets that unease as inauthenticity.

The truth is you cannot go stale even with copious rehearsal, as long as you show up for the presentation with energy and focus. That is the key. You cannot be completely energised and focused if you do not know what you are doing.

3. Look over the heads of your audience.

In many different articles and courses, I have come across Communication Experts who recommend looking over the heads of audience members to help ease your nervousness. This is a mistake because making and maintaining eye contact is an important part of connecting with your audience.

In the words of William Shakespeare, "Our eyes are the window to our souls." It is no surprise that we connect with each other through them. Eye contact also helps you establish trust with your audience. Effective speakers look at a few people, one at a time. This creates a relationship, and it is less intimidating to share your message with each person than it is to a large crowd.

4. Put more emphasis on your slides.

Most presenters think, "If my PowerPoint is great, my presentation will amaze them." They spend time adding photos that tell the audience nothing they do not already know, and add animation which only makes the presentation longer.

Preparation means more than putting in countless hours on an enticing slide show. What you say and how you say it are more important than your slides. For example, in his famous speech, I Have a Dream, Martin Luther King Jr. won the hearts of his audience with his passion and authenticity. Do you believe the same impact can be achieved with the use of clichéd stock photos? Of course not. Unless slides are necessary for sharing data, leave the PowerPoint at home.

5. You have to grab people's attention at the start.

The public speaking world adopted this principle from advertisers who face the challenge of distracting us from our busy lives so that we will read or watch their ads. The situation is quite different when you are presenting or speaking in the public arena, because people are sitting in the audience waiting for you to start. They may be talking to the person next to them or checking their phone, yet, as soon as you begin, they will listen to you. The challenge in public speaking is not as much in the grabbing of attention; rather, it is in retaining it. In those first key moments, the imperative objective is to establish rapport with your audience.

CHAPTER 10
IN CONCLUSION

| **Chapter 10 -** In Conclusion |

I hope that reading this book has helped you see why the ability to speak in public is such a valuable skill for you to acquire. Also, that even the most fearful, uncomfortable speaker can become a great one with some work and practice. The rewards for presenting well are numerous, especially when you realise that almost every business conversation is a presentation to some degree. It is all about communicating with other people in a way that shows you are passionate about the subject of the conversation, and why it is important to the people listening to you.

The biggest deterrents to becoming a great speaker are a lack of self-confidence and a fear of rejection. However, these are things that you can work on. There are many successful strategies for relieving speaker's anxiety and taking command of the stage. In my experience, fully preparing and practising your presentation are what it takes to make you a master communicator.

Start by knowing your Purpose - which is, in the most simple of terms, to solve a problem or fulfill a need for your audience. Focusing on the people to whom you will be speaking and understanding that your role is to help them, rather than to merely entertain them, eases speakers' anxiety. Researching the "players" and their roles within an organisation helps you better empathise with their individual goals and structure your speech so that it addresses the specific needs of the key decision-makers.

People love speakers who are connected to their subject matter emotionally. Find your Passion and concentrate on that. When you are passionate about the topic, you carry that enthusiasm through to your audience which, in turn, makes them more interested in what you are saying or recommending. Before reading the chapter on Passion, you may have thought, "That's fine for giving speeches, but what about presenting at a business meeting?" Remember, you may not be passionate about the organisational changes you are explaining, or even a new product being considered for market.

However, you can be passionate about what that means for your company, the consumer or your own career. Regardless of the topic, being passionate about it also lessens any fears you may have about speaking on it because you will know it forwards and backwards.

The steps included in the Preparation phase also make you a more confident speaker. Becoming comfortable with and practising vocal nuances and body movement, and learning how to use all the tools in a speaker's toolbox, ensures that you will express your passion to its fullest. Your audience will remain engaged with your talk because of the rapport and passion you bring to your speech. Having complete control over the subject will change or enhance the audience's impression of you. Rather than being just another salesperson or marketer, you will be perceived as an expert giving necessary advice.

When the day arrives, you will be ready if you have practised and practised. You will know your material and feel confident in your message. You will eliminate potential "hiccups" by checking all the technology and getting familiar with the room in which you will be speaking. And, importantly, you will know how to release any leftover tension through visualisation and breathing exercises.

These are steps that anyone can use to their advantage. Some will find it easier to work on them alone than others. If you are looking for help over and above the friends and family you invite in as your practice audience, you may find it extremely helpful to work with a coach like myself.

If you are looking for help with your presentations and delivery, please get in touch with me, **Lis@WinningWithWords.ca**

| Free Special Offers |

Do you want to work with a mentor and get help to achieve more with presentations and delivery? Or, do you want to know more about the principles and practices I have shared in this book? I am offering two very special promotions only to the readers of my book.

| FREE GIFT |

An audio programme filled with even more advice, strategies and tactics for becoming a great presenter who sells their ideas, products, and recommendations such as a professional speaker.

FREE AND PERSONALISED 30-MINUTE CONSULTATION WITH ME

Visit **www.WinningWithWords.ca**
or email **Lis@WinningWithWords.ca**

www.ingramcontent.com/pod-product-compliance
Lightning Source LLC
Chambersburg PA
CBHW071209200326
41519CB00018B/5444